COMIC RELIEF™

edited by
TODD GOLD

introduction by
Bob Zmuda, President, Comic Relief

AVON BOOKS ◆ NEW YORK

VISIT OUR WEBSITE AT
http://AvonBooks.com

COMIC RELIEF™ is an original publication of Avon Books. This work has never before appeared in book form.

AVON BOOKS
A division of
The Hearst Corporation
1350 Avenue of the Americas
New York, New York 10019

Comic Relief credits the following people for the cover photos: Jay Silverman (Louie Anderson); Andy Hayt/HBO (Billy Crystal, Whoopi Goldberg, and Robin Williams; Dennis Miller; Gary Shandling); Ira Margolin/HBO (Bob ''Bobcat'' Goldthwait); Richard Howard/ HBO (Paula Poundstone); Patrick Harbron/HBO (Rita Rudner).

Library of Congress Cataloging in Publication Data:
    Comic relief / edited by Todd Gold.
        p.   cm.
        1. American wit and humor.   I. Gold, Todd.
PN6161.C6577   1996   96-22851
791.45'6—dc20   CIP

First Avon Books Hardcover Printing: October 1996

Printed in the U.S.A.

FIRST EDITION

QP   10   9   8   7   6   5   4   3   2   1

Dedicated to
Billy Crystal, Whoopi Goldberg, Robin Williams,
and Chris Albrecht,
and in memory of Andy Kaufman

Board of Directors

Bob Zmuda, President
Dennis Albaugh, Vice President
Jack Shakely, Secretary
Chris Albrecht
Dr. Joe Greer, Jr.

Board of Governors

Pat T. Lee, Co-Chair
John Moffitt, Co-Chair
Jeff Berg
James Blancarte, Esq.
Larry Brezner
Bernie Brillstein
Michael Fuchs
Sandy Gallin
Brad Grey
Barry Josephson
Buddy Morra
Jack Rollins
David H. Steinberg
Sandy Wernick

ACKNOWLEDGMENTS

Thank you to the Comic Relief staff: Caroline Thompson, Mario Bernheim, Bibbi Herrmann, Mary Ruth Koogler, Mike Miller, and Kristin Young.

Also thank you to the past and part-time Comic Relief staff: Judd Apatow, Paul Bennett, John Davies, Linda Goldman, Bob Kelty, Mark Kogan, Craig Hoffman, Suzanne Lauer, Tod Mesirow, Craig Minassian, Christy Sinickas, Andy Stein, Tambi Stollman, Dennis Walto, Artie Weitz and Jeff Wilber.

Many thanks to Comic Relief's corporate friends: AAA Flag & Banner; ABC/CapCities; American Airlines (Pat San Pedro); American Video Group; Avon Books (Lou Aronica, Stephen S. Power, and Joan Schulhafer); Bacardi; Canada Dry; Castle Rock Entertainment; Chronicle Books (Beverly Ornstein); Claridge Hotel, Chicago (Michael); Columbia Pictures; Comedy Central; Complete Post, Inc.; Coopers & Lybrand; Evan M. Greenspan, Inc.; Fleet Mortgage Group; Fourway Communications (Hank Shaw); Hard Rock Cafe; Hearst Entertainment; Henley Park Hotel (Josette Sheldon and David Hill), Washington, D.C.; Hollywood Novelties; Igby's Comedy Cabaret; Joe Robbie Family & Stadium Staff; L.A. Auto Show (Andy Fuzesi); L.A. Cellular; Ladd Limousine (Jeff & Lisa); Laffy Taffy; Levy, Pazanti & Associates; Los Angeles Clippers; Los Angeles Lakers; Louise's Trattoria; Magnet Interactive; Mayflower Hotel, New York City (George); The Mint (Jed Ojeda); Mitchell, Silberberg & Knupp; Motivational Fulfillment; NBC; National Basketball Association; New Line Home Video; Nike; Palm Restaurants (Wally Ganzi, Bruce Bozzi); Pepsi-Cola; Procter & Gamble; Radio City Music Hall; Royal Caribbean Cruise Line (Richard Fein); Rhino Home Video (Richard Foos); George Schlatter and staff; Showtime; Spring Air Mattress Co.; Sprite; Star Trek (Rick Berman); Steiner Electrical Industries; Theatre Authority (Judy Bailey); Tommy Tang (Sandy Tang); Tropicana Twister; Universal Color Lab (Sam Oh); Universal/MCA Pictures (Ron Meyer); Warner Lambert-Certs/Rolaids; The Waylan Company (Bill Schmidt).

And thanks to the many friends of Comic Relief: Gerry Abrams, Susan Abramson, Mark Adkins, Hal Altman, Army Archer, Charles Audia, Olivia Ayala, Arthur Badavas, Linda Baer, Bob Bain, Diane Barnett, Gabe Bartalos, Maria Bellu-Colonna, David Bender, Rachele Benloulou, Larry Bird, Gary Blasi, Esq., Carolyn Blitz, Bill Bohnert, Tom Boles, Mayor Tom Bradley, Keven

Bright, Ellen Brown, Bonnie Burns, Brad Cafarelli, Cristi Catlin, Melissa Cheek, Tony Clifton, Andy Cohen, Fritz Coleman, Becky Conti, Brent Cook, Rick Cramer, Hollace Davids, Richard Davies, Gigi Delmaestro, Danny DeVito & Rhea Perlman, Dian Dingman, Farm Aid Staff, Carole Feld, Jeff Frankel, Esq., Jan Frazier, Bud Friedman, Beth Gold, Todd Gold, Fred Goldey, Larry Goldman, Wendy Gruell, Marc Gurvitz, John Hamlin, Bonnie Hathaway, Ron Herman, Bill Herrmann, Doug Herzog, Steve Hewitt, Caroline Hirsch, Carrie Hollister, Michael Iskowitz, Laurie Jonas, Lisa Kane Clark, Vic Kaplan, Michael Kaufman, Stanley Kaufman, Michael Katz, Marvin Katz, Linda Keeler, Senator Edward M. Kennedy, Rick & Carol Kerman, Gil Kerr, Nancy Kurshner, Diane Jakacki, Charles Joffe, Earvin "Magic" Johnson, Michael & Juanita Jordan, Rosalyn & Deloris Jordan, John Landis, Joe Lauer, Tom Leonardis, Marleah Leslie, Nancy Lessor, Jared Levine, Michael Levine, Jerry Lieber, Arnold Lipsman, Rick Ludwin, Brenda Lynn, Mancow, David Martin, Susanna Martin, Michelle Marx, Stafford Matthews, Esq., Marty Mickelson, Paul Miller, Walter Miller, Jimmy Miller, Jon Miller, Lynn Margulies, Ray Manzella, Mara Mikilian, Molly Miles, Melody Miller, Roger Moley, Monique Moss, Graham & Susan Nash, Willie Nelson, Rick Newman, Andy Nullman, Sally Nussbaum, Rick Pallack, Judy Pastore, Susan Patricola, Michael Petok, Rikki Poulos, Rob Reiner & Michael Singer, Ray Reo, Mayor Richard Riordan, Danny Robinson, Michael Rotenberg, Ellen Rubin, Toby Russell, Mark Ruttenberg, Rich Ruvelson,

Tim Sarkes, Sal Scamardo, Tom Scott, Quentin Schaffer, Howard Schatz, Glen Schwartz, Ruth Schwartz, Tod Schwartz, Barry Secunda, Rich Siegel, Emily Simonitsch, Nancy Severinsen, George Shapiro, Hank Shaw, Roger Sherman, Esq., Mitzi Shore, Wendy Smith, Nicholas Spill, Arthur Spivak, Mike Stoller, Carolyn Strauss, Dan Strone, Alfred Thimm, Jr., Isaiah Thomas, Steve Thomas, Jeff Thorsen, Joe Troiani, Sonny & Pam Vaccaro, Bruce Vilanch, Robert Wachs, Jeff Wald, Tom Wescott, Howard West, Vanna White, Leah Wilcox, Marsha Williams, Mark Zacharin, Laurie Zacks, Bill Zehme, Alyssa Ziegler, Sophie & Chester Zmuda.

In memory of Marty Klein and Lee Stevens.

One more special thank you to Michael Fuchs, Bridget Potter and Jeff Bewkes.

And many, many thanks to Home Box Office and its incredibly supportive staff who believed in Comic Relief from the beginning.

And finally nothing would happen on the front lines without the National Health Care for the Homeless Council and its Executive Director, John Lozier, and the many staff and volunteers at the twenty-five health care projects in twenty-three cities.

Acknowledgments

TABLE OF CONTENTS

Table of Contents

INTRODUCTION

On March 29, 1986 Billy Crystal, Whoopi Goldberg and Robin Williams hosted the first Comic Relief. Televised live on HBO, the four-hour-plus fundraiser for the homeless featured Hollywood's brightest stars. From the start, their punchlines hit a politically edgy bull's-eye. "How would you describe the homeless?" Whoopi asked. "Judging from the present administration's policy of trickle down," Billy answered slyly, "I think they're being pissed on."

And so it went. Michael Keaton, Richard Dreyfuss and Penny Marshall made heartfelt pleas for greater awareness of the problem, while Garry Shandling, Paul Rodriguez, Dennis Miller, Bob "Bobcat" Goldthwait and dozens of great comics from Howie Mandel to Minnie Pearl filled the stage with their greatest bits. And behind the scenes, chaos reigned as stargazers like Carl Reiner and Pee-wee Herman were blinded by a pair of full moons when Harry Anderson and Joe Piscopo dropped their pants.

The good humor of so many great comics impressed George Carlin, but he still voiced a concern we all had by asking, "Is anyone going to watch?"

That was the biggest question. It hovered over us like a humorless network censor. Despite three exhausting months of persuading comics to rearrange their schedules, rehearsals and prayer, none of us knew if anybody cared. Helping the homeless wasn't the hippest charity in town. Nor was it the most politically correct. Would the show's audience, we worried, resemble the one for the midnight slot at a comedy club? Two drunks and the bartender, waiting it out till closing time? Was anyone going to tune in?

And if so, would they actually pick up the phone, call our 800 number and pledge money to help the homeless?

Sixty minutes into the show our fears were erased. Billy walked onto the stage and exclaimed, "The phones are going nutso! We're getting $10,000 a minute!" The show was a smash. The entire country loved it. By evening's end, we had raised $2.5 million and dramatically increased awareness about an important issue.

Now it is ten years later, and Comic Relief is stronger and more visible than ever. But that is a mixed blessing. It is shameful, comic Robert Klein once noted, that an organization like Comic Relief is necessary so people can eat, sleep and receive medical care. These are the basics. Food. Shelter. A doctor. Warmth. Security. The things most of us take for granted. Yet the homeless population continues to grow. Corporations downsize. Jobs disappear. Mortgages eat up paychecks. Savings go toward unforseen bills. It happens, and suddenly one of us becomes one of those other guys. Misfortune doesn't care whether you wear a blue collar, a white collar or a V neck. In 1980 a TV news anchorwoman lost her job and not long afterward found herself living in the street. Norman Cohen, a forty-one-year-old man who had worked dependably in construction for twenty years, was laid off and ended up homeless.

"Without an address or a telephone, it's tough to get a job," he told us.

Unfortunately, such complaints have turned into a haunting chorus. "I served in Vietnam," one homeless veteran said. "For what? For me sleeping in the streets?" Another woman, a mother, said, "There were times I just wanted to roll over and die. I feel rejected. Like no one cares."

That's where Comic Relief comes into play. The ever-growing ranks of good, hard-working but displaced individuals and families on the streets, like Norman Cohen, like the Vietnam vet, like all the others, illustrate how important it is that we exist. In the past decade, Comic Relief has staged seven HBO telethons, numerous related special events and raised more than $35 million. But don't get the idea this solves the problem.

"Tragically," Robert Klein noted during Comic Relief VII, "thirty-five million dollars is just a drop in the bucket. We've only been able to purchase four homes."

Just kidding.

The money goes directly to providing health care for the homeless in twenty-three major cities. So far more than one million needy people have benefitted.

But as Whoopi said in Comic Relief VI, the Reagans have gone away but the homeless haven't. There are between two and three million homeless people in America. According to recent studies, families with young children constitute the fastest growing segment of this population. How we respond to their need, Louie Anderson observed, is a measure of our own humanity.

It is easy to help.

How easy? As Robin once explained, lots of people paid forty bucks several years ago to see John Wayne Bobbit's penis on a pay-per-view TV special. For only thirty dollars, though, they could have bought a Comic Relief T-shirt. The stitching is better and it doesn't shrink in cold water. Plus, the money helps the homeless.

I don't know what I was thinking when the idea for Comic Relief first flashed in my brain. I wanted to do something, and I asked myself what? What could I do? I'd missed out on that internship with Mother Teresa. Quincy Jones wouldn't let me sing on "We Are the World." My only experience in aid-related humanitarian work was as a writer for the late Andy Kaufman. I helped make people laugh. As a result, I got pretty weird reactions when I told people about my idea of gathering all the great comedians for a gigantic fundraiser similar to what rock musicians did in Live Aid. Everyone said, "You're nuts."

Fortunately, I didn't know if that was an insult or a compliment. Neither did Chris Albrecht, HBO's president of Original Programming and Independent Productions and Comic Relief's patron saint. Years ago Chris and I had a comedy act together. So he knew I was nuts. But he also said HBO would adopt Comic Relief as its own. Not only did that decision team Chris and me in the comedy biz again, it gave Comic Relief the credibility to attract Billy, Whoopie and Robin as our hosts. And once they signed on, all the other comics climbed aboard.

"Whoopi called and said, 'Do the show or you're finished in the business,' " Paul Rodriguez told me with a joking grin. But then he added a serious, compelling reason. "My parents were migrant workers. We moved around a lot. I've known hardships. It's nice to give back to people you can see." I also remember the late John Candy saying, "Some events are important and you just want to take part." And the following year, Louie Anderson, one of eleven children raised in a housing project, confessed that one of his brothers might be living on the street. "But for a stroke of luck, it could be any of us," he said.

When Robin showed up at the Union Rescue Mission in downtown Los Angeles, a homeless man told him, "You sure didn't find no new jokes today." At the privately funded House of Ruth, a shelter for women and children in Washington, D.C., Whoopi offered hope to mothers and babies. And at a shelter in Seattle, Washington, Billy listened to factory workers, Vietnam veterans, parents and children describe how a factory could close, related industries move to other states and how seemingly overnight, a few hundred homeless could turn into a few thousand. "Tell them we're not all bums," one young man said to Billy. "Tell the people we're not happy in this situation."

The stories we heard were heartbreaking. In one shelter, a little girl, typical of so many we met, described how hard it was to play at a friend's house after school, all the time thinking about how she no longer had a home of her own. "It makes you sad," she explained tearfully. She wondered why people didn't care more about each other, why some people had to go hungry and without doctors, and then she added, "Me and my mom want to get out of this place so we can have a home of our own and be happy."

Comic Relief aimed to turn such dreams into reality. Only one month after Comic Relief I, we delivered a brand new van to the House of Ruth. A bag lady received emergency medical treatment that saved her from otherwise losing a leg to gangrene. A darling little girl, written off as too slow to learn to read, saw a whole new world open up after an eye exam and new glasses.

In Denver, Paul Rodriguez helped open a medical facility made possible by funds from Comic Relief. He was approached by a woman holding a baby. She said, "If it wasn't for Comic Relief, this child wouldn't have been born."

I recall touring Chicago's Firehouse Annex, a home for alcoholic and battered women. My guide, a soft-spoken woman, explained how money raised by Comic Relief had enabled the Firehouse Annex to take in a violent, alcoholic woman, slowly give her responsibilities and build up her self-esteem, until she cleaned up and got a regular job.

"What a wonderful story," I said. "Can I meet her?"

"You're talking to her," she replied.

Such stories have made Comic Relief a trusted part of the social fabric and inspired us to branch out beyond the HBO televents. Our many fundraising efforts include: *A Comedy Salute to Michael Jordan,* which aired on NBC in 1991; the marathon nine-hour *Hurricane Relief* that brought much-needed immediate relief to areas of Florida, Louisiana and Hawaii after powerful storms devastated both areas of the country in 1992; the Fox network's one-hour special *Baseball Relief,* which united comedians and baseball players in 1993; NBC's *A Comedy Salute to Andy Kaufman,* a tribute to the comic genius whose death inspired the founding of Comic Relief; A&E's twenty-four part series *The Best of Comic Relief,* which has raised significant funds and awareness; and our most recent fundraiser, the five-day *American Comedy Festival,* celebrating Comic Relief's tenth anniversary and broadcast by ABC in May, 1996.

Our efforts have paid off across the country. In New York, for instance, the funds raised by Comic Relief paid for a support group for homeless sufferers of AIDS. In Chicago, we renovated a building that now houses a medical clinic. In Birmingham, we refurbished a development center for pre-school homeless children. In Los Angeles, Comic Relief funded specially designed drug treatment programs and counseling services for homeless families. In Philadelphia, we paid for the services of a pediatrician who provides care for homeless children in family shelters. We have been able to help people in similar ways in cities from Milwaukee to Phoenix.

Each year we hope it won't be necessary to continue, but as comic Paul Rodriguez once observed, "There's something wrong when the richest, most powerful country in history has a guy named Bob sleeping on a manhole cover." So as long as the need exists, Comic Relief will be back in some way, shape or form. Homelessness is a serious problem, but Comic Relief has turned it into a laughing matter. We've shown that where there's laughter, there's hope. It bears repeating.

Where there's laughter, there's hope.

This book, our latest project to result from that spirit, is a collection of the funniest routines performed by comedy's superstars during the seven Comic Relief tel-events. Special thanks go to HBO's Chris Albrecht, Michael Fuchs, John Moffitt and Pat Tourk Lee and the

many other wonderful people who have had a hand—
often two hands—in making Comic Relief such a
success.

But most importantly we thank the comics. This
book, whose proceeds will go directly to Comic Relief, is
a credit to both their genius and generosity. Not only is
it the mother of all comedy books, it can also double as
a pillow, roof or seat cushion, depending on the need.

Upon finishing, it might also inspire some of you to
ask what you can do to help. Which is good. Because
that is exactly how all of this began.

Bob Zmuda
President, Comic Relief
1996

Welcome to Comic Relief—the book.

As you read these pages, you will be entertained. You will learn about the homeless. You will laugh. You will be moved. You might even be outraged.

Oh geez, now it sounds like a conversation with Marlon Brando.

But don't worry, it's not.

The following pages contain some of the best material from the greatest collection of comedians assembled since . . . well, since the Simpson jury.

Of course, Billy, Whoopi, Robin, and the others did this for charity. Most of the jurors ended up getting paid.

Ah, well . . .

Don't panic. The jokes get better.

And hopefully the homeless problem will, too.

Why Comic Relief?

"Have you seen a family of eight living in a station wagon?" Robin asked dozens of journalists who assembled for the press conference announcing the first Comic Relief. "Well, have you? Have you seen a sixteen-year-old wino wandering around Venice beach? Have you been to Chicago and seen a guy living in a paper box? Or have you wandered around New York and seen people who've been turned out from the mental institution out on the streets? Just go to any city. You'll catch it."

Why Comic Relief?

Studies dated from 1985 reported between two and three million people homeless people in America. A year later, the demand for emergency shelter increased in virtually every major city in the country. People from all backgrounds comprised the growing population of homeless: women, children, underemployed and unemployed families. The median age was between thirty-three and thirty-five. Some thirty to forty percent were veterans. Nearly forty percent were women and/or children under the age of fifteen.

Why Comic Relief?

"There are families here," Whoopi said. "We're doing a benefit, here in America, to raise money for family."

Why Comic Relief?

"Basically, we're trying to make a lot of moola for people who are homeless," Pee-wee Herman explained.

From seeing Minnie Pearl stand beside Bobcat Goldthwait (who later showered onstage) to hearing Howie Mandel describe how his goldfish succumbed to a bladder infection—"I didn't know it was urinating thirty-seven times a day until its bowl tipped over, full"—Comic Relief's debut on March 29 produced many memorable moments, but nothing came close to matching the final tally on the old tote board. By the end of the four-hour marathon, Comic Relief had taken in $2.5 million. We had, as Pee-wee hoped, raised a lot of moola.

Then we put that money to work in various cities. Vans were purchased to provide hot food, medical supplies and other assistance to over five thousand homeless people under bridges, in parks and in other isolated spots. Physicians and nurses were added to clinic staffs. Clincs were expanded, medicine bought and distributed, and social workers hired. In only a matter of months, we made a difference, alleviated some pain and offered up some hope.

In short, Comic Relief was no joke.

1-(800)-528-1000

GARRY SHANDLING

Sonny Bono ran for congress—and won. How lucky could we get?

I was actually thinking of voting for the Captain from Captain and Tenille.

At least he had military experience.

I've never run for president.

I've thought about it, and the only reason I'm not—I swear to God—is that I'm scared no woman would come forward and say she had sex with me.

I can see it, though.

I'd be giving an interview on CNN, looking into the camera and saying, "Come on, Susan, you know you fucked me."

No reply.

"Well, I counted it as sex!"

I met a new girl at a barbeque. A very pretty blonde girl, I think. I don't know for sure. Her hair was on fire.

And all she talked about was herself—one of those kinds of girls. "I'm hot and I'm on fire."

You know the type.

"Jesus Christ, help me! Put me out! Come on, could we talk about me a little bit?"

These days you have to be married or have a steady girlfriend because you can no longer have casual sex.

Of course, I have never believed in casual sex anyway.

I have always tried as hard as I could.

No woman has ever said to me, "Hey, you're taking this casually." That's because I usually wear sweatpants. I have black cork I put under my eyes. . . .

There are all these new phases regarding sex. In an article in *Newsweek* I noticed the phrase "sexually illiterate" used in some context.

I didn't understand.

What does that mean, sexually illiterate?

Does anybody's penis read?

I would like to know.

Mine doesn't.

It will look at pictures. But I have never seen it yawn and put a bookmark in.

I work out all the time.

I work out everything but my ass.

I don't work out my ass because I don't think about it. I don't.

That's the truth.

But these days there is all this pressure in society that your rear end has to look great, too.

Forgive me, but I never think of it. I never even see my ass unless something has gone horribly wrong.

To me, it's a safety device to prevent me from falling in the toilet.

So as long as it's doing its job, I don't have to make it look attractive, too. That's just a little too much pressure.

I flew to Arizona to visit my grandmother, who's in her nineties. She still drives. People hear that and say, "God love her."

But no one will get in the car with her.

"No, we don't need a ride, Ada. We'll just hitchhike."

She has a 1962 Dodge Dart.

It has the push-button transmission.

At this point, it's like a damn slot machine. She's hit so many motorcycles, there are stencils of motorcycles painted on the side of the car. It's like a fighter pilot.

She's a hero at the nursing home.

Many youngsters dream about what they'd like to do with the rest of their lives—become a fireman, a nurse, a baseball player, an activist, a television person. It's a child's privilege to dream. But some children do not have that. They live in an environment of fear and desolation. Their minds are occupied with survival—plain, ordinary survival. The life of a homeless child is marked by much pain and suffering.

When you deprive a child of the right to hope and dream, you take away not only a piece of his future but of all our futures.

—NORMAN LEAR

ELAYNE BOOSLER

If my parents lived with me now, I'd get even for my childhood. I'd make them sleep in separate bedrooms. My mother would say, "What? Are you crazy? I've been sleeping with this man for years."

I'd say, "Look, I don't care what you do on the outside. But when you're in my house. . . ."

All my mother does is clean. She loves to clean. She says stuff like, "Look at this! You could eat off my floor."

You could eat off my floor, too.

There are a thousand things down there.

I never understood what kind of claim to fame it was to be able to eat off someone's floor.

"You know what? We had dinner at the Booslers'. We ate off the floor."

"Oh, yeah. We were there and we drank out of the toilet. What a hostess."

Life is short. I don't care about the floor.

I take vitamins. They drop and roll under the refrigerator. I don't pick them up. I have years of vitamins under the refrigerator.

I'm going to come home one night and find a six foot roach saying, "I feel good!"

Forget what you have heard about being unmarried. It is still fun being single. You just have to be more careful. You have to think about your own welfare. For instance, you can test people before you date them. That's all you have to do. Have them come to the door and say, "Hi, ready in a second. I'm just sewing this button on my jacket." Then you have a slight accident. A little slip. "Oops, I just pricked your finger on this slide."

Single women used to go out looking for really hip, cool guys who look like they know what to do.

You know what we are looking for now? A file clerk who looks like he has not been laid in 15 years. "Hey there, Baldy, you've never seen a nude woman? Great. How're you doing? Can I buy you a drink?"

I think it's terrible that TV stations won't advertise condoms because of pressure from religious groups. Isn't that ignorant?

Wouldn't it be great if we found you could only get AIDS by giving money to television preachers?

Television preachers are amazing. They say God talks to them. Right. God talks to them and they can only get a show on cable?

Oh, I say all this with love.

There is one ad on TV. I see it all the time. But it's the wrong approach. It shows a woman looking into the camera and she says, "It's not worth dying for."

Well, that's not going to work. Because when you are in the act, it kind of is worth dying for.

If they want to sell condoms, they should be more positive. The ads should say, "Look, buy condoms and you'll stay up for years."

I did notice that they have moved condoms in the stores. They are no longer behind the pharmacist's head. Now they are up at the register. Along with the other impulse items. "Will that be everything?" the checker asks.

"Yeah. Uh, no. Uh, yeah. Uh, no."

I have always liked the idea of impulse items. Things you realize you *must* have before you leave the store. What do we have for impulse items now? Gum, *People* magazine, condoms, keychains . . .

"Let's see," I say to myself, "I'll offer him some gum. I'll get laid. And we'll talk about nothing but the home."

You stand at the checkout counter, buying your stuff, and there's all those boxes of condoms. And since there is nothing to do while waiting, you read the condom boxes. They are pretty funny, too.

Elayne Boosler

Do you know what Trojans say? "New shape." I didn't know this was necessary. Must have been that Chernobyl incident.

Another box said, " Reservoir." I said, "You mean these things can actually generate hydroelectric power?"

Then I noticed they have goatskin condoms. "What's the deal on these?" I asked.

"They feel more natural," came the reply.

"Well, not to the girls up north," I said.

How about the names they give condoms? Trojans. Ramses. Pharaoh. Are you going to get laid or conquer Egypt?

If they want people to use them, they should make them funny. They should have a little sign on them that says Baby on Board. Put that annoying sign right where it belongs.

Condoms are not the big deal everyone makes them out to be. Not as embarrassing as we think. Anybody can look cool putting on a condom. Just open it up like Errol Flynn. Be a swashbuckler. Put it on and great events will follow.

Of course, there is probably not a guy in America who can look cool taking one of these things off.

Women know. Whatever they say, they are thinking, Ah, just go out, do it in the next room.

I don't think there is a woman left in America who has a wicker wastebasket in her bedroom anymore.

I have a steel-belted radial wastebasket with my address painted on the side. The truck just backs right into my bedroom that day.

COMIC RELIEF

Everyone is in the baby business these days. Even the Vatican. The Vatican came out with a new rule. No surrogate mothers.

Good thing they didn't make this rule before Jesus was born.

The Pope is a hard guy to please, isn't he? No weird sex. Well, what's this kiss my ring stuff?

One of my favorite things to do is walk around New York City. I can do this for hours. It fascinates me to no end. It is also pleasurable for me. I do it by choice, and when I am finished I can go home. There used to be a store at 57th St. that sold the most expensive sheets in the world. They were like $10,000 for a set.

I walked in and asked why they were so expensive. The saleswoman explained that they were comfortable. "But why so expensive?" I asked again.

"They have a very high thread count," she answered.

"Oh," I said. "High thread count. Sure."

Then one night I was walking by the store and saw a homeless man sleeping right in front of the store. He was on the sidewalk. But he had a smile on his face.

Boy, those sheets really are comfortable, I thought. They are so good you only have to be close.

These days crime is really terrible. I live in New York. I have six locks on my door. They are all in a row. But when I go out I only lock every other one.

I figure no matter how long somebody stands there and picks the locks, they are always locking three.

I think there is so much crime because there is so much tension. I was crossing the street in some city. I happened to be in front of a man's car as the light changed. He had to wait one extra second for me to get by. Still, he yells out his window. "Whore!"

I looked at him and said, "What a memory!"

I think men and women perceive crime differently. If a man gets mugged, he loses his watch or his wallet and that is about it.

Women have other considerations. I remember once when I was walking in New York with a boyfriend and he said, "Gee, it's a beautiful night. Let's go down by the river."

"What? Are you nuts?" I asked. "I'm not going down by the river. It's midnight. I'm wearing jewelry! I'm carrying money! I have a vagina with me!

"Tomorrow," I added, "I leave it in my other pants. Then we'll go down."

Men mean well, but they all say the same thing. "I'll protect you."

"Oh, thanks. You have the easy job. They kill you instantly. Then I have to boogie with Jim and Ray till dawn. Nah, I don't want to go."

Boyfriend. This is such a weird word. There's no good word about someone if you are not married. Even calling a guy you live with your boyfriend makes you sound eleven years old, doesn't it? There is just no good word.

Old man? If you are not living with Willie Nelson, that one doesn't work. It is hard to introduce him.

So now I just say, "Hi, this is my cousin who thinks he loves me and he can't make a commitment. He was married a long time ago. The divorce wasn't nice. They split the house. Now he's hanging out with me. . . ."

I think it is hard to live with another human being. If you are married or living with someone, then there is one thing that gets said day and night that drives both of you absolutely crazy. But one or both of you always say it. And do you know what it is? It is what. "What?" The word, the phrase, the implication, the irritation.

"What?"

"You're deaf?" you mumble.

"What?"

"I don't mumble, stupid."

"I heard that."

"That you heard."

These days politics is pretty hard to understand. Pretty depressing. I got worried when the conservatives gained such a stronghold in the government. They don't understand about the separation between Church and State. I get very nervous when these same people want to take sex education out of the schools. Most conservatives want to take it out. They believe that sex education causes promiscuity. In other words, if you had the knowledge, you'd use it. But hey, I took algebra and I never do math.

I remember President Bush speaking out against abortion. When asked why, he said it was because birth was a miracle.

Well, popcorn is a miracle, too, if you can't figure out how it happens.

Bush was amazing, though. He was against abortion, but for capital punishment. Spoken like a true fisherman. Throw it back. Kill 'em when they're bigger.

There are so many conflicts over religion. Why? All people are pretty much the same anyway. There's only one difference between Catholics and Jews. Jews are born with guilt, and Catholics have to go to school to learn it.

What's with the NRA? They don't want to outlaw automatic weapons. I guess you have to understand where they are coming from.

They feel it's okay to shoot a human as long as you eat the meat after.

And remember the whole controversy about whether or not women in the service should be in combat? Can women fight? Can women kill?

Yeah, I think so.

Just have the general come over here and say, "Hey, see the enemy over there? I just heard them talking. They say you look fat in your uniform."

They say we will never have a woman president of the United States. They say we are too erratic to run a country because our hormones change once a month and it makes us crazy. Yeah, right.

If a woman was president, she'd be like this: "Get over here! That's right, I'm the president. Are you nuts? You take hostages on a day when I'm retaining water? I can't believe I have to sit here and waste my time with a morally bankrupt terrorist like you when there is a sale on and the stores close at six!

"Send in the Exxon idiots. Get in here. You had to clean up the coastline and you couldn't do it? You should have sent women. It would've been clean in a week, for crying out loud. You only sent men. How are they going to get oil out of the ocean when they can't even get their socks and underwear off the floor?"

Men in power always have their sex scandals. Women in power never have sex scandals. You know why?

There are no women in power.

Who could have a sex scandal?

We don't even have a word for male bimbo.

Oh, okay—senator. But still . . .

BILLY CRYSTAL
(As Fernando)

You know, my darlings, Fernando here. You know, last month I visited this town, this town that was a little cardboard city. It was all these boxes stacked up on the street. Large boxes, small boxes. Boxes, my darlings. One next to the other. And looking maybe like the set of a summer stock play someplace.

But it was not summer stock, my darlings. It was not a play.

It was real.

People actually lived in those boxes.

And I went down there, my darlings, to talk to the homeless people because I had been misinformed.

I had thought the homeless were those involved in the making of *Heaven's Gate.* But goddammit, I was wrong.

Fernando is this crazy Katzenjammer type of guy.

What did I know about the homeless?

I had no idea.

But darlings, I interviewed some of these people, and as I talked with them I was moved. After listening to them, and talking some more, something came over me. Something came over Fernando. I know what you're thinking, darlings. No, it was not Sandra Dee that came over me.

I put my hand in my pocket—and I can tell you this, it's hard for me to put my hand in my pockets, darlings, when the Sansabelt is twenty-nine inches and the waist is thirty-four, if you know what I mean.

Then I pulled my hand out, darlings, which wasn't easy either.

And I gave.

You see, I helped.

Yes, my darlings, Fernando helped.

And let me tell you this. Listen to me, darlings. Listen to Fernando. After I gave, after I helped, it was one of the few times in my fabulous life when I realized it was better to feel good than to look good.

And darling, I felt *MAHHH-VELOUS!*

We now have a subculture that's made up of the disenfranchised, destitute and painfully unprotected families for whom the American dream has turned into a nightmare. The majority of them live on the streets because they've run out of options. Or maybe they've run out of their last two paychecks. A substantial number of people did all the right things. They went to work. They raised a family. They put away money for a rainy day. They never imagined they would ever be without resources.

But there they are—in shelters, living out of abandoned cars. Wondering how it all happened.

It could be anyone.

—DUSTIN HOFFMAN

"There are still far too many homeless people out there who still need our help!" Billy declared at the opening of Comic Relief II.

And so the comedy troops, led by Billy, Whoopi (who beamed in via satellite from New York), and Robin gathered for a second time. The televent raised over $2.5 million, another spectacular success. In just two years Comic Relief had raised more than $5 million. Almost the entire sum was immediately distributed to the twenty-three Comic Relief supported Health Care for the Homeless project sites across the country. We continued to reach out quickly and effectively. A shelter in Cleveland was able to purchase a van. In Nashville, a warehouse was converted into a health care facility. A clinic in Milwaukee expanded its outreach program, targeting families living in cars and unsafe, abandoned houses. From New York to San Diego, Comic Relief funds provided health care and vital services to men, women and children.

In short, Comic Relief worked.

Billy and Robin ended the show with a set of instructions to ensure Comic Relief kept on working:

- Every time Michael Jackson visits a plastic surgeon, send ten dollars to Comic Relief.

- Every time you hear someone use the word *impact* as a verb, impact them on the frontal lobes and send twenty dollars to Comic Relief.

- Every time you see Bill Cosby in a commercial, send ten million dollars to Comic Relief.

- Every time you hear the word *meltdown* applied to something other than a nuclear power plant disaster, send thirty-five dollars to Comic Relief.

1-(800)-528-1000

If you're stuck with a loser at a singles bar, you can always excuse yourself and go home alone. But if you're stuck in a life-threatening situation when you live on the street, there's no place to go because you are home.

—PENNY MARSHALL

LOUIE ANDERSON

My dad didn't like people as much as he liked his car. He even introduced it to people. "It's my Bonneville," he said. "My family's over there."

Then he went on. "It's an American-made car. You can drive it head-on into a train and live."

That was my cue to mutter, "You ought to try that, dad. The seven-fifteen's coming around the bend."

"Don't get smart with me," he growled.

That was my favorite expression of his. Don't get smart with me. Just once I wanted to make a weird face and go, "Duh! Is this dumb enough for you, dad?"

When I was a kid getting to borrow the car was a big deal. "Hey dad, can we use the car?"

"Take the Rambler," he said.

"Dad, I raked the lawn. I cleaned the garbage. I built the new addition."

"Well . . ."

Then I had to lie.

"Where are you going?" he asked.

"Around the block," I said.

"How many kids are going?"

"Just half a kid."

But before he handed over the keys, he gave you a lecture. "Now I'm not giving you this car so you can screw it up."

"Well," I said to myself, "then I don't want it."

After getting the car, though, I picked up my friends. Three hundred people jammed into the car. And that's when I turned into my dad.

"Don't smoke dope in here!" I screamed. "My dad's a musician. He'll know."

I would drive around town. At some point, I'd get a little overconfident and turn goofy. That's when I hit that tractor.

"You didn't even know you were in a field, did you?" someone said from the backseat.

All my friends left.

"Good luck, Louie. See ya."

Then the guy from the station came out. The guy whose name is always Smitty. The guy who always has the same look in his face.

"This your dad's Bonneville?" he asked. "What'd you do, hit a train?"

I shrugged.

"Listen, Louie, I know your dad. Why don't you go in and lay under the hoist and I'll crush your legs."

For a minute, I thought, That's not bad.

But then Smitty pulled the car free. The fender was twisted. I drove the Bonneville home with it scraping on the wheels. I pulled up in front of the house and saw my dad in the rocking chair in the front window. The scene from *Psycho* flashed in my mind. I parked with the smashed side facing away from the house, thinking that in the middle of the night Dean Jones would come by and put flubber in there. Some miracle would occur. Then I walked in the house and threw the keys on the table.

Why not? They're of no use anymore.

Then my dad realized I was home a little early. "You better not have screwed up that car or you won't be driving it anymore," he said.

I muttered, "You won't be driving it anymore either."

I was always surprised when my dad really reacted. I thought I was sure to be killed. But he went, "Well, that's all right, Louie. How do you think that pink door got on the Bonneville."

"I don't know."

"Anyways, we're going to work on that together. We're going to fix it. You and me. Every Saturday. Every minute of your free time we're going to spend working on that car."

"Couldn't I just make payments or something?"

I never wanted to work on the car with my dad. I didn't know anything about tools and he wasn't really a mechanic. But he jacked up the car, then got underneath and I handed him tools. "Give me that nine-sixteenth wrench," he called.

I looked. I couldn't find it. I gave him the whole set. "Here, take them all."

After I little while, I knew what was going to happen. He hit his knuckle. Then the tools came flying out.

"Nine-sixteenth—incoming! Watch out!"

Then he blamed me. "Get out of my life!" he screamed from under the car. And that's when I looked down at that jack and thought, "College or prison?"

I might as well talk a little about the homeless.

People don't like the homeless. We used to. We used to drive by the homeless and wonder what we could do to help. Now we say, "Lock the doors."

I think most people would rather help them. But these days you can't even suggest it. You're driving by a homeless guy and say, "Should we pick that guy up?"

"No, he could get up if he wanted to."

"But he's only got one leg."

"Well, he shouldn't have fallen down then, should he?"

I try to have compassion for the homeless. I have a brother living on the streets. He's one of them. I keep wondering if I'll drive by somewhere and see him.

So I've seen my share of homeless. Most people don't like the homeless because they don't have a home. If people didn't have to look at them, then maybe they'd get a better shake. But only one thing bugs me about the homeless.

They've got all the good shopping carts.

I don't mind, though—as long as they help me get my groceries. Just bring the cart. Let me use it a few minutes.

Drunks are the people who give me problems. They always have something to say. The more they drink, the more they want to give you a little philosophy.

"Hey, Louie. Life! Live it!"

Great, aren't they?

Then they pass out. Their head falls on the table and they're gone. But as soon as you pass a bottle or two under their nose, they wake up long enough to say something stupid.

"Hey, watch it! My friend Louie here will kick your ass."

But as soon as they get outside, watch it. They come alive. Did you ever notice that?

"I'm driving!" they say.

And then once you're in the car, they all get the same idea. "Let's eat!"

Drunks always want to eat, and they get mean about it. They threaten you. "I want to eat. Or else I'm driving."

Then they walk into a restaurant as if everyone was waiting for them. "Hey-hey-hey! We're here!"

"Hey, lady," they say, walking by the first booth. "Can we sit with you? No? Well, then how 'bout a fry? Can I get a fry? Just one fry? Ah, ya cheapskate."

They always order a big thing of food, a mountainous

plate, but when it comes they eat one fry and pass out. Later, they wake up with food all over their face, stinking like alcohol and garbage and fried food. They have no clue what has happened. In fact, they think they've had a great time.

And so they all say the same thing: "Life! Live it!"

I went through a period when I watched a lot of television. I got cable, and then I got that bad cable habit of clicking through the channels. Just click-click-click. Really fast. You just stare at the changing picture and go, "No, no, no, no, no . . ."

"Wait a minute! John Davidson! What the hell is he doing?"

"He's in Hawaii, selling something. Oh, geez, what the hell is he selling?"

All the big stars from my parent's generation are on cable selling things. Like Ed McMahon. My mom and dad loved him. Now he's selling insurance policies to the elderly, asking them to send in $7.95 out of their last eight dollars for a policy that will leave money to children who don't visit them. And Art Linkletter selling this chair, a special adjustable chair. I don't know anyone who has ever seen one in anybody's home. If they did, they'd walk up and try it for about ten minutes.

"Maybe it's good if you're laying in it and you drop something."

The worst product I have seen offered on TV is that

COMIC RELIEF

medic alert thing that you talk into. "My foot is stuck! It's really stuck! Ugghh!

"Now I've fallen. I've fallen and something's on top of me. Call Art Linkletter. I'm stuck in his chair!"

I've been trying to be a human being. A better human being. It's a difficult task. People don't want you doing that. I've been doing it for years, and people just keep kicking my ass. I like to hug people, but people don't like being hugged. Especially in Los Angeles.

You hug someone and they look at you like, "Oh, no, wait a minute. What the hell was that? Is that legal?"

"It's a hug."

"Oh, Christ. Don't start that."

PAULA POUNDSTONE

I once stayed at this lovely Holiday Inn in Florida. As you probably can guess, when you're in show business a while you only get the best.

I went to check in and noticed a sign on the wall. It said, "This is a drug-free workplace."

I thought, Why are they giving us this information. It just seemed odd to me. This is a drug-free workplace.

Two years ago did they have a sign that said, "The bell staff is as high as a kite."

It just seemed odd to have the virtues of the staff right up there on the wall. "Many of our staff read."

Thank you, Holiday Inn.

I used to work at the International House of Pancakes. I know what you are thinking. How's that possible? Why? But you set your goals and go for them. It was a dream. I made it happen.

It was the worst job I ever had in my entire life. When people were rude to me, I touched their eggs. It's true. I flipped them over in the back with my hand. Four times. They didn't know, but I felt better.

People complained all the time about the service. We weren't slow. The floors were sticky. We were stuck in the back trying to get to the tables.

One time I tried getting a job at a submarine sandwich shop. Only they wanted me to take a lie detector test just in order to apply for the job.

I said, "What the hell am I going to lie about in a sub shop?"

Did they fear someone would ask for roast beef and I'd say no. "How much is the tuna?"

"Thousands."

My mom is one of those really angry moms who gets mad at absolutely everything. Once when I was a little kid, I accidentally knocked a Flintstones glass off the kitchen table. She said, "Well, dammit, we can't have nice things."

My mom had a range of two emotions: she was either pissed or trying to get you to feel bad for her. That was it.

As a kid, she told me how she learned to swim. She got in a boat and someone took her out in the middle of a lake and threw her into the water. That's how she learned to swim.

I said, "Mom, they weren't trying to teach you to swim. When they shot at you, they were trying to teach you to deflect bullets."

One of the weird things about crime nowadays is that you can be a criminal and no one seems to care anymore. Remember that 560-pound criminal who was released from jail because he had asthma? He claimed jail was bad for him. Who made up this rule?

I thought jail was supposed to be a little bit bad for you.

Apparently not anymore.

Apparently now it's like, "Sorry, claustrophobia. Can't go. Wish I could. Sorry."

The electric chair? "No way. Even a heating pad gives me a rash."

It seems they will let almost anyone go. The guy who shot Robert Kennedy, Sirhan Sirhan. He goes up for parole every year. Once he even told the parole board that if Kennedy was alive today, he would speak in his favor and say, "Let him go."

What a tough break, you know? The one guy who would have supported him, and he shot him.

Women have one helluva time getting dressed these days. Everything has big puffy shoulder pads. I don't know why we have to have that.

Paula Poundstone

I'm waiting for big huge butts and big huge thighs to come into fashion.

My shoulders were the one area of my body I felt were okay in clothes. As it turns out, they aren't big and huge and poofy enough. I usually wear both a shirt and a jacket. Sometimes they both have big, huge, poofy shoulder pads. I look like I have mountains under my ears. People talk to me. I can't even hear them. "I'm sorry," I say, "but if you could speak directly into the valley, it would be helpful."

And if you send them to the dry cleaners just once, they come back looking like big, huge, poofy *deformed* shoulders.

If you don't get them on just right when you are getting dressed, it looks—just for a second—as if there is someone behind you. I can't even remember how many times I have frightened myself while alone in my own apartment. I defy anyone to tell me why we have to wear these things.

Someone once explained it was to make our hips look smaller.

Oh, I don't think I'm fooling anyone.

In 1990, Comic Relief was held in New York. It gave me the opportunity to ride the subway for the second time in my whole life. People always told me that the New York subway was real scary. I didn't find it scary. I thought it was a little odd, in fact. Everywhere I looked were big signs that said, No Spitting.

I don't know if I have a big defiant streak in me or what, but I never even thought about spitting till they brought it up.

And then it was all I felt like doing.

Somehow it activated my saliva. Oh, great, I thought, where am I going to spit?

These days you can't fly anymore without the pilot pointing out various landmarks outside the window. Personally, I don't want to see the stuff out the window. Nothing out the window is exciting to me. I just want to sleep. Besides, I don't think I've ever seen anything they have pointed out. The pilot could tell me there are clouds and ocean out there and I'd be like, "Oh, hell, I don't see it."

And if the thing is on the left, I'm on the right. If I'm on the right, then the thing is on the left. Something like that.

If it's only on one side of the plane, then why tell everyone?

Just tell the people on the left, for heaven sake.

The pilot should get on the intercom and whisper, "Psst. People on the left. Psst. This is the pilot. Don't tell the people on the right, but there is the coolest stuff out the window right now.

"Don't all look at once.

"Psst. People on the left. We hate the people on the right. You are the best people on the plane right now. Look at them, just sitting there. God, I hate them. They're ruining everything.

Paula Poundstone

"Psst. We're purposely flying crooked now so they can't see stuff.

"You don't have to put your tray tables up if you don't want to."

Every four years elections roll around. But sometimes I think we are too immature to have elections. Maybe we should just give it up and do what it appears we do anyway. We could get a big auditorium, and then anyone who wants to be president—no, any man who wants to be president, because apparently women are big losers. We just can't do it. Forget about us.

So any man who wants to be president would come stand on stage. Say, there are ten of them. They line up on stage. And then anyone who has had sex with them has to come and stand right behind them. And they have to come that night. They can't come ten years later and say, "Oh yeah, I had sex with him." They have to come that night.

And then the man with the least amount of people behind him, the man who clearly has had the least amount of sex, may be our leader.

For some reason, people think it's an important measure of character whether or not our politicians have had affairs. Like the controversy with Clinton.

But the fact is I don't think this comes within striking distance of our top thousand problems. If I thought having sex with a politician could solve any of our problems, I'd volunteer to do it. And I don't even like sex.

And I am so sick of every guy who's up for political office saying they *experimented* with drugs. Unless there's a lab coat and data involved, it was not an experiment.

I don't even care about drugs. I care about honesty. I think that's the important thing.

Be an adult. Take responsibility.

What's happened to people?

If I'm pulled over with drugs in my car, I hope I can say, "But officer, I'm in the laboratory. I can't roll the window down. It will affect the variables."

"Are you sterile? I can't let you in unless you're sterile."

I don't think so.

One of the biggest problems we have these days in this country has to do with gun control. We have an epidemic of gun-related violence, and we can't seem to get any effective legislation to stop it because the National Rifle Association is one of the most powerful special interest groups in Washington. They keep using the same lame old argument: "Oh, it's the Second Amendment. The Second Amendment gives us the right as Americans."

Well, first of all, the Second Amendment gave us the right to bear arms in order to have a ready militia. It's not for traffic incidents.

Paula Poundstone

Maybe the guys who wrote the Constitution didn't know about assault weapons. Maybe they were thinking about the kind of big, heavy guns you have to load with gunpowder, pound with that long metal thing, then aim and so on. It takes about fifteen minutes. The other guy has time to run away. Of course, there are some people who disagree. They argue the Founding Fathers were visionaries. They knew what the future would be like. They knew about assault weapons.

Okay. I'll give them that.

But how about they were wrong about the Second Amendment?

There. I said it.

I don't know why we continue to revere without reservation the Founding Fathers. They were not right about everything.

They had slaves!

They wrote the Constitution during a hot, sweaty summer in Philadelphia and they still wore layers upon layers of clothing. They were sweating to death under those powdered wigs.

They were not right about everything. It's just a theory.

But who am I to criticize anyone, including the Founding Fathers, about being a parent?

I remember when I first got my foster son. He was the cutest little guy I'd seen in my entire life. Friends were surprised that I'd get a baby. As I changed him, I was surprised by how much I liked it. I always knew that

I'd be responsible. I knew that I'd do what needed to be done.

But there was always that little voice in the back of my head that said, "Remember, the saxophone was in the closet after a month."

*For a hungry, homeless child there are no opportuni-
ties. Not unless someone like you is willing to care.*

—CHER

*E*lizabeth and Billy moved their family cross country hoping for a better life. But someone broke into their van and stole everything they had.

Billy:

"I never in a million years thought I could be homeless. Then here you are, 2,500 miles away from anyone you could possibly turn to, and I can't even describe the feeling of hopelessness."

Elizabeth:

"I never had to worry about where the next meal was going to come from or where we were going to sleep or what we were going to do. I never imagined myself homeless. I've always worked. I've always had money.

And today we don't have a penny. The kids are hungry. We ended up sleeping in the van."

Their Children:

"They worry about something happening to me and my brothers and sisters. They worry that we wouldn't get something to eat or find a place to live. And it feels scary because they're much older than me and they're braver than me, so if they're scared then it's going to make me even more scared.

"The hardest thing about being homeless was when we didn't have any food or anything. If I could help, I'd go hungry so the rest of my family could eat.

"When we were walking down the streets, I didn't feel safe even when we were with my parents.

"When I'm at school, I look like everybody else. But when I come home, I'm not like everybody else.

"I wish we could have a house and be happy like we used to be."

1-(800)-528-1000

COMIC RELIEF

Homelessness can be a temporary condition. But only if we are willing to give them the tools to get off the streets and back into society.

—Los Angeles MAYOR RICHARD RIORDAN

BILL MAHER

At least we have a government that's a little sympathetic to homelessness. You have to remind yourself that we had Bush, and we had Reagan. God Bless him.

Ronald Reagan came from show business. His idea of how the government should help the homeless was like your agent.

"We'll try to get you work. But don't bug us about it."

So you have to put that in perspective.

We survived the 1980s. Back then, the economic program was called *trickle down.* That actually meant they were pissing on you.

How much closer can you get to saying that without using the words?

Trickle down.

The whole theory was this: We have all the money. If we drop some, it's yours. Go for it.

But that's not the way to solve the problem of home-lessness. No, you solve it if everybody in the country would focus on it. We can do that. It's possible. It's been done before. In World War II. That was the only time. But we did it. Once. Everyone throughout the country shared the same thought, the same collective opinion about one big problem.

Nowadays people don't believe it's possible for every-one to think the same way, but I disagree. We've come damn close again.

You don't believe me?

A few years ago, I swear to God, everybody in America was thinking the same thing again: What does Michael Jackson's dick look like?

Is it a tattoo that's got him in trouble?

Is there a pattern?

Does it look like Diana Ross?

So it's possible, right?

But it's getting harder. Soon we'll have access to five hundred TV channels.

Great.

Nobody will have anything in common.

As a country, we're in a difficult position right now. Look at the reports of the last census. Did you catch this?

They added up all the people in this country who con-sider themselves a minority and it added up to more than the population of the country.

That's a bad sign right there.

These days everybody's a victim. You listen to the

name of things we take for granted. We hear them all the time. They're meant to evoke sympathy.

Prisoner of fame. Oh, what a grisly thing that is, huh?

Prisoner of Turkey. Now I think that's a bad thing to be.

Eating disorder. That means sticking your finger down your throat.

To me, an eating disorder is starving, not having any food, not having any choice. That's a disorder involving eating.

Throwing up after lunch is just very American.

How about *emotional rape?* There's one. He forced his opinions on me.

I think everyone just has to grow up a little and realize that, hey, life's tough for everybody. It sucks across the board.

"Hi, I'm Bill, and I'm a birth survivor."

I've got to live with that every day.

Here's a thought, though: If everyone's a victim, then nobody's really a victim. You know what I mean?

It's true.

Everything that used to be a sin is now a disease. It used to be that if you sinned, you went to a priest and he made you feel guilty about what you'd done. He said, "You *schmuck* . . ." Well, he didn't say that exactly. But that's the idea. You confessed your sin. It was done.

Now people go to a psychiatrist. Psychiatry. I'm not knocking it, but psychiatry was invented for people who are really nuts and now it's just for anybody who's whining about how they can't get laid or how they got locked in the closet with a spider when they were three years old.

Oh, shut up.

Grow up!

Even if we could find the spider now, what good would it do?

And psychiatrists are no help. What do they tell you? "Well, we'll have to get back into your childhood to find the trauma."

Who can't find the trauma in childhood?

"I'm two feet tall. I don't know what the fuck is going on. Everybody can beat me up."

"Gee, doc, you're a genius to find trauma there."

Psychiatrists also hand out these drugs like Prozac and Halcyon and Valium. I say why not just take mushrooms? You know, God made something naturally. Of course, I'm not advocating mushrooms. I just don't understand why the government acknowledges the fact that some people need something to change their bad mood, but that the only way to do it is by choosing a drug on their list.

Why? God made mushrooms. They're natural. I don't know who's making Prozac, but God made the mushrooms. Does God make mistakes?

I don't think so.

Why are there so many different kinds of mushrooms, and one kind that's really different?

It's like one mushroom is good in sauce, one is good on eggs, and then this special one makes you laugh for eight straight hours.

That doesn't seem random to me.

Because God knows that sometimes you have to laugh for eight straight hours.

God knows life sucks. It's right there in the Bible. Look at the book of Job. The book of Job is all about Job asking God to take away pain and misery.

And God says, "No, I can't. But I'll give you drugs. That's the best I can do. I'll give you drugs, but I can't take away pain and misery because then no one would talk to me."

Please. I'm paraphrasing, but these are the basic sentiments.

Let's face it, God has a big ego problem.

Why do we always have to worship Him?

"Oh, you're the greatest. You're perfect. We're fuck-ups. You know everything. We're in the dark."

Secure people don't need to hear that all the time.

I believe Dr. Kevorkian is onto something. I think he's great. Because suicide is our way of saying to God, "You can't fire me. I quit."

BOB SAGET

I'm a resident of California, which means one thing: earthquakes. But people in California just don't care about earthquakes. They are apathetic.

"Oh, look, the ground's opening up. Oh, there goes my house. There goes my wife and kids. My car! Oh, crap, my Beamer! How am I going to get to work?"

"Oh, there goes work!"

"All right! Party!"

I'm just scared there's going to be a major earthquake at the time I'm getting a vasectomy.

I have three daughters. Which means I'm in trouble.

When they're sixteen, I'm going to install Lo-Jacks in all their panties.

I'm scared. I want to know where they are, where those panties are going.

Three daughters and people ask, "Were you upset that the third child was a girl?"

I say, "No, not at all. I'm whittling a boy out of wood right now."

My oldest daughter was two years old when my wife got pregnant with our second child. It was great news. We were trying to have another kid.

Well, she was trying. I just laid there.

I'm also an incredible lover. Just ask the cable guy.

Actually, my daughter looks just like the cable guy. It's a problem. It really is. But we get free HBO, so screw it. What the hell?

In truth, I'm worried abut all these 900 numbers that come on the cable channels. My daughter is very smart. Gifted, in fact.

Consequently, I'm worried that when she gets a little older I'm going to get a phone bill and ask, "Honey, did you make these 900 calls?"

And she'll say, "Yes, daddy. I've been bad. Spank me, daddy. Spank me real hard. Spank me good, daddy."

"Where'd you learn that?" I'll ask. "Which number was that? I just want to know so I can call myself."

The best device we have in our house is the baby intercom, a kind of walkie-talkie that lets you monitor your kid from other rooms. So my daughter's in the crib with one part of the intercom, and I'm in the other. Then, all of a sudden, I hear her crackling over the static:

"Breaker, one-nine. Daddy, I've got spit-up on my shirt and I'm packing a load. Please, come help me out."

Sometimes I have trouble getting out of the house at night. My wife and I are about to leave and my youngest daughter doesn't want to go to bed. She says, "Sleep with me. Sleep with me." She says it over and over again.

It upsets me. You know why? I flash forward 20 years and picture her saying it to another guy.

I have this interesting story. It happened back when *Full House* was still on the air. The show, which ran for years, also starred Dave Coulier and John Stamos. John had worked previously on *General Hospital*, which I mention only for background. Here's the good part:

So one day John and I are on the way to *Full House*. We are driving to work, and as we make a left another woman comes from the opposite direction. She's not really smart. But she really was fine afterward. I have to say that at the outset. But she was making a left at this corner and didn't see a bus coming. It was fifteen feet from her—in her blind spot, I guess. That little strip between the windshield and window.

Anyway, the bus hit her car and spun her around three times. I immediately made a wish, which is customary when I see something spinning. I wished she'd be okay.

Then I got out my video camera and got some great blooper footage. No, that's not true. I don't get off on violent videos.

The woman was laying in the middle of the intersection in her car.

John was amazing. He was like Batman. He opened up his briefcase, took out a cellular phone and handed it to me. "Bob, call 911!" he said.

Then he hopped out of the car. He stopped traffic and said, "I'm not a doctor, but I've been with some on television." He ran over to her car. He put it in park. He took over. He was amazing.

Meanwhile, I was trying to find the switch on the phone. I had no idea how the thing worked. I looked at it. I couldn't find the nine. I thought, Well, maybe I should get one of these things, but I don't know. It's a dollar-fifty per call. Is there a pay phone nearby? Finally, I got the phone on. I thought, Maybe I should order a pizza. With all the excitement, I'm kind of hungry. No, that's not true.

Then I ran over to the car. John was looking in the window. He turned to me and said, "Bob, I did all the action stuff. You talk to her. You can't shut up."

No problem.

So I leaned into the car, looked in her eyes and said, "You're going to be fine. Just breathe normally. We're on at eight o'clock on Friday nights."

Just kidding. I didn't tell her to breath normally.

As it turned out, she was fine once she realized she hadn't died and gone to sitcom hell.

Not only do I think we have to do something about the homeless problem, I believe we can. You can. I can. We can all do something to make sure they aren't hungry.

We can go to my mom and dad's house. My parents are willing to feed everyone in the world.

They just want everyone to pick a date because they have to defrost.

Actually, sometimes you don't want to eat their food. You want to cut out the middle man and throw that shit in the toilet.

That's not true.

What you really want to do is bury it.

My father is amazing. He's between seventy and ninety-eight years old, but he looks fourteen. He works out. He's in incredible shape. And mentally he's still exceptionally smart. One day, he taught me something very valuable. He took me aside and passed down some of his wisdom.

He said, "If, at the end of your life, you can count all of your friends, your really good friends, on just one hand, then you've been spending a lot of time alone in your room."

That's what he told me. And his hand was in his pants when he said it.

I'd like to talk about the sex I have with my wife, but when you're married you're not supposed to say, "Hey, I did my wife last night."

It's okay if you're in a bar and say, "See that chick over there? I did her."

People go, "All right. Good for you."

But if it's your wife, they don't want to hear about it and you aren't supposed to talk about it. It has to do with respect.

Actually, my wife is a very fortunate person. Because if I'm videotaping us having sex and she falls out of bed, she can win $10,000.

Anyway, what's weird for me now is my three-year-old came in and saw me getting out of the shower. I was naked.

She said, "Daddy, what's that?"

She thinks it's a towel hook.

But my six-year-old is actually the real problem. I walked in on her while she was reading a story to the three-year-old.

I heard her say, "Once upon a time a man came and he took the baby away and everybody lived happily ever after."

We watch movies together. I remember when we watched *Peter Pan*. My six-year-old came up with a beautiful question.

She said, "Daddy, how does Captain Hook wipe himself?"

That was so sweet. My first thought was to tell her that he just rips himself a new asshole. But I had no idea.

"Smee does it," I told her. "He yells, 'Smee, wipe me.' "

Children are gifted with the ability to imagine just about anything. This natural gift is nurtured in many ways. In fairy tales, ghost stories, cartoons and super heroes. Nothing is too far-fetched for the young minds to absorb. All is grist for the mill of imagination. But what happens when the child becomes the center of a story that is not of her making? What happens when a child is faced with a life situation that is beyond her ability to even imagine? What happens when the unimaginable happens?

—Susan Sarandon

*T*he HBO Radio Network proudly presents the biggest broadcast of 1989. Brought to you by Ollie North Shredded Wheat, the cereal shaped like tiny documents. . . .

And so began Comic Relief III, our biggest fundraiser yet. Whoopi described it as "business as usual." Robin exclaimed, "The good news is we're back. The bad news is we still have starving people." And Billy led the audience in song: *"Don't be a greedy little bastard/Those yuppie days are over and gone/Forget the lame excuses you have mastered/It's time to throw away the Perrier and Gray Poupon/America's the union of the hero/ That's why we're here . . ."*

The message got through. Some four hours later, Comic Relief had taken in a record $5 million, almost as much as the first two televents combined. In addition to raising money, we were also raising the awareness of unpleasant, sometimes life-threatening situations being experienced by so many homeless people, enough to call it a national crisis. As one mother explained:

"Being homeless with five kids is really, really hard. Sleeping in the car is very frightening. You don't really sleep. What you do is try and get your children asleep and then you just watch, and everytime there's a shadow coming up behind you you get really frightened. You don't know if someone's gonna harm you or what."

Through the gift of laughter, Comic Relief opened people's hearts and minds to this grave problem, and then showed it was possible for them to do something about it. That February, Comic Relief presented a check for $150,000 to the Los Angeles Homeless Health Care Project. Comic Relief funding also helped open a new health care facility in San Antonio. Similar activities took place in Alburquerque, New York, Seattle and other cities across the country. We joined forces with Second Harvest, a national food bank. And, Shelly Long and Bob Zmuda represented Comic Relief at the U.S. Conference of Mayors meeting on homelessness.

In three fast-paced, productive years, Comic Relief had become synonymous with helping people attain a basic right to safe shelter and health care.

People were pulling together.

People were making a difference in the lives of others.

1-(800)-528-1000

Like everyone else, I know I'm guilty of spending too much money on things I don't really need.

My last credit card bill was so big that before I opened it I actually heard a drumroll.

But there is a solution. Next month put a donation to Comic Relief on your credit card. You won't feel guilty when you get the bill. You won't say, "Oh, my gosh."

—RITA RUDNER

STEVEN WRIGHT

I want to get a tattoo over my whole body—but taller.

This morning I woke up out of a dream and I went right into a daydream. I was having a dream that midgets were trying to assassinate me.

So I bought a bullet-proof car. And since they were midgets, I bought a convertible.

If you shoot a mime, should you use a silencer?

Babies don't need a vacation. But I still see them at the beach.

It pisses me off. When no one's looking, I'll go over to a baby and ask, "What are you doing here? You haven't worked a day in your life."

Once I walked all the way across Texas looking for my dog. I walked from one state line to the other, and when I got to the other I noticed my dog was behind me the whole time.

When I was in the middle of the desert a UFO landed. Three one-inch-tall guys got out. They walked over to me. I said, "Are you really one inch tall?"

They said, "No, we're really very far away."

My friend walked his dog George all at once. He walked him from Boston to Ft. Lauderdale and back. And then he said, "Now you're done."

One night my friend wasn't home and I went over to his house and broke in. I went up to his dog and put little contact lenses in his eyes that had cats on them. The dog flipped out all over the place.

Then I took one out and he ran in circles.

I was five years old and watching TV when I saw the commercial that said, "Only YOU can prevent forest fires."

Oh, no.

Every night I crawled out the window with a bucket of water.

My uncle was a clown for the Ringling Bros. Circus, and when he died all of his friends went to the funeral in one car.

I'm living on a one-way, dead-end street. I don't know how I ever got there.

I've been getting into astronomy, so I installed a skylight. The people who live above me are furious.

I've been making wine at home, but I'm making it out of raisins so it will be aged automatically.

It doesn't matter what temperature a room is. It's always room temperature, right?

Driving hasn't been the same since I installed funhouse rearview mirrors.

I remember the day the candleshop burned down. Everyone just stood around and sang Happy Birthday.

It's 1966. I was in Little League. I was on first base. I stole third. I ran straight across the diamond. Earlier in the week, I learned the shortest distance between two points is a straight line. So I ran. I argued with the ump that second base was out of my way.

About a year ago my girlfriend was on the pill and using a diaphragm and an IUD all at once. Recently she had a baby. The baby was born wearing armor.

Steven Wright

I wear eyeglasses during the day. Yesterday I was walking down the street wearing my eyeglasses and all of a sudden my prescription ran out.

I bought some land. It was kind of cheap. It was on somebody else's property.

The guy who lives across the street from me has a circular driveway, and he can't get out.

I know what it's like to do funny stuff. I also know what it's like when you don't have a real place to live at night. I'd rather try to be funny.

—WHOOPI GOLDBERG

WHOOPI GOLDBERG

I want to talk culture right now. You know, black woman to mostly white women. When your man comes home smelling like some chick, you all say, "Come on in, it's all right. It's okay, get into bed and go to sleep."

We don't do that shit. See, we'll put your ass into the microwave. We don't care. We won't just kick your ass, we come prepared.

We do our nails.

We get dressed up.

Remember Brenda Richie? It's a while back, but you remember when Brenda caught Lionel with another woman?

She was dressed, honey.

She did her hair.

She got in the car.

She went over and found her man.

And then she beat Lionel's ass so bad he thought he was back in the Commodores.

Oh, shit, I've got my ass kicked in a marriage a few times. I married this one guy just because I felt like I was getting old and shit was dragging. Gravity had got ahold of my shit. No question. I pulled them up and they fell back down.

I thought I might as well get married.

So I married this really pretty young guy. He could not fuck to save his life. It cost me money to get laid badly.

That pissed me off.

Nobody wants to talk about sex. The real frank shit. But I don't give a shit. I'm going to talk about sex.

How about oral sex?

That's one of those things that causes people to get very uncomfortable. But I love it because you can't get pregnant. You can't. There's no way.

They didn't tell me that back in high school. If they had, I would have been totally gone.

Sex is a strange thing. I like it. When my daughter was growing up I'd tell her sex was wonderful.

Not too long ago I became a grandmother, so I guess she listened.

At first I worried about Bill Clinton. He made me nervous. I wanted to hear him say that he smoked pot. I would've liked to have heard him say, "Yeah, I smoked a couple of joints." Because then this shit about him having a mistress comes up and you start wondering what he's going to say. What if the press asked him, "Hey, Bill, did you give your lady head?"

"No. I tried it for a second, but then I spit it out."

That shit made me nervous.

But then came the year of the dick. The year when everybody's dick was in the news, from Bobbit to Clinton. And it thrilled me that Bill Clinton's dick was making headlines. It really did. I was overjoyed. Because I want a man in the White House who can fuck. I fuck. You fuck. He should fuck, too.

I love a good stiff one, but I was so glad to see that Bobbit woman even up the odds. Women live with the knowledge that shit can happen at any point. You turn down a dark alley and someone grabs you. It ain't no party, baby. But after she cut it off, men suddenly had to think about shit like that. It gave them pause. And I didn't think Lorena should have suffered any consequences for doing what she did.

She could've been a bitch about it. Instead she told them where the dick was.

I wouldn't have told them.

I would've said, "Find it, motherfucker. You're so attached to it, see if you can sniff it out."

Let's talk about men who've been in the news over the past few years:

There was Clarence Thomas. Him and Anita Hill. Stupid shit. All Clarence had to do was look at Anita and know she wasn't giving up shit. Take a look at the woman. She's not a player. You don't mess with a woman like that. They don't take messages in Coca Cola cans lightly.

Then there was William Kennedy Smith. Now please. This guy doesn't deserve to have sex. But hey, women who hang with Kennedys need to know that this family ain't the Clevers. You know? It's three in the morning, and when they come home they want to do one thing—they want to fuck.

And what about Mike Tyson? He went to jail. That girl busted his ass. But what the hell was she doing in his room at three in the morning? Because this is not new information, like one day he was sweet and the next day he wasn't. The man's an animal. Where were those chaperones?

But the strangest has been Michael Jackson. Maybe I'm crazy, but here's my big question: After he was accused of doing whatever to those kids, there were like five hundred people coming out of the woodwork saying they saw everything. Well, if they did see something, then their ass needs to be in jail, too. Why didn't they stop that shit?

In any event, I don't know whether Michael did or didn't do anything, and I hope he didn't, and my gut belief is that nothing happened. But it's getting hard to take him seriously when he's sitting up on TV with eyelashes and makeup on. He's saying, "Trust me," but looking like Liza Minelli.

I don't even want to talk about the guy in the Bronco. That shit is over. They did what they did—fuck it.

It's all interesting shit.

The thing that's really got me insane is the abortion issue. People go nuts over that. I'd like the names of all the anti-abortion people so that when all those kids start having babies we can take them to their house.

I was also thinking about how for the past year the government has been about to go under financially. They're broke. They ain't got any cash. All we hear is that the government has this big debt. But then a thought occurred to me. Who the fuck do we owe a trillion dollars to? What the fuck did we buy?

What did we spend it on?

I know what we didn't spend it on.

We didn't spend it on education. I remember reading how a bunch of high school kids were asked to define the Monroe Doctrine and they thought it was a new band.

They didn't spend it on welfare. Shit, there'd be nobody on welfare if there was a trillion dollars passed around out there.

And they didn't spend it on medical care. If they had, there'd be no need for Comic Relief.

It's scary times, baby. The sci-fi movie has begun.

Whoopi Goldberg

They want to dismantle everything that Ronald Reagan and George Bush didn't take away. They want it all. Children, education, welfare, medical care.

Read the news and you see shit like how there's no money to feed kids at school. Why can't we feed the kids at school? Where the fuck is that trillion dollars going?

People have to wake up. Every cut they make is going to kick our ass later on. We have to watch them. We have to be ready.

Ask yourself, baby, do you know what's going on? Are you ready?

L IVE FROM NEW YORK, IT'S . . .

That's right. Like a traveling circus, Comic Relief IV hit the road, broadcasting from Radio City Music Hall in the heart of New York City, which Robin called "the greatest piece of Japanese real estate this side of Tokyo."

"The city's got a new name," Billy offered.

"Yeah," Robin answered, taking the bait. "It's called Nissan North."

All kidding aside, Comic Relief IV could only be called one thing—unbelievable. The show raised over seven million dollars, breaking all sorts of records for effort, enthusiasm, excitement and *money.* Comic Relief made sure it was all worthwhile.

In May, Robin and Whoopi testified before the Senate Labor and Human Resources Committee in support of a bill benefitting homeless men, women, and children. "George," Robin said in reference to President Bush, "read my lips. Help us."

But there was much more, particularly on the street, where it mattered most. In Miami, Comic Relief helped double the size of Camillus Health Concern, a clinic anchoring the Health Care for the Homeless Project, where special attention was given to caring for homeless children. In Boston, we funded optometric care and immunizations. We began an AIDS education program in Milwaukee. Other services were added or expanded in Chicago, Cleveland, Phoenix and additional cities. And on July 10, we noted with great sadness the passing of Mitch Snyder, head of the Community for Creative Non-Violence and the nation's leading advocate for the homeless.

"The next time you see someone out on the street, don't pass them by," Snyder once said in an attempt to summarize his approach to a problem that seemed to confuse and confound even the brightest and best-intentioned lawmakers. "Say hello, ask them how they're doing, get them something to eat. Just tell them that you care, tell them that they're human beings. And I think that's what I would ask of anyone."

1-(800)-528-1000

Imagine what it must be like for a child in the streets. A child without a home or protective parents to comfort him. Imagine living in constant fear, facing constant rejection, even being scorned by your peers and put at the mercy of a merciless environment. And these are the most vulnerable of God's creatures—the children, the innocent, the helpless. More and more show up on the streets. We must not let it happen to them.

—DEMI MOORE

PAUL RODRIGUEZ

I have a bit of an identity problem. I'm like the only Mexican who hasn't won the California lottery yet.

But so what. Bigger things piss me off. Like whites in Volvos who have Baby on Board stickers in the back window and believe this gives them the right to cut in front of you on the freeway. "Get out of the way, goddammit. I've got a baby on board, and you don't even have any lights."

Even worse. I hang out at Venice beach a lot and there are just too many Iranians there. It's not that I'm against them. But these people are hairy. They've got hair in places monkeys don't. I'm not lying. They've got hair on their chest, their back, on their buns . . . I'm talking Winnie the Pooh. I'm talking Chewbacca.

And it's like people who've got a lot of hair on their

body think the rest of us, who are normal, are jealous. We're not, dammit. We're not.

And the hairier the person, the smaller the bikini underwear they have on. I can't figure it out.

I would do anything for the homeless. Give them money. Whatever. You know why?

Because I don't want them moving into my house.

The worst thing about being homeless is that you'll never be able to enjoy camping. If you don't believe me, ask a homeless person.

"Hey, pal, you want to go to Yosemite? Sleep under the stars tonight?"

"No, fuck you. Take me home."

Mexicans don't camp. That's one thing we don't do. We don't go camping in the woods, especially during hunting season. We'd be mistaken for a deer.

Somebody would go, "Your Honor, I saw brown skin and brown eyes. He had his hands up. I thought they were antlers. I shot his ass."

Certain sports are not ethnically conducive.

I admire white people for coming up with bungee jumping. What kind of drug were you on when you came up with that? Where's the fun?

If you ever see any Mexicans hanging upside-down from a bridge with their feet tied, call the cops. Someone is trying to kill us.

And you'll never see two Vatos up on a mountaintop going, "Check out the powder."

If you see any blacks or Mexicans on top of a mountain, call 911. There's been a plane accident.

The majority of homeless people are poor whites, Hispanics, blacks and Native Americans. I've never seen a homeless Japanese person.

There's nobody out there named Song Lee.

They're too busy buying art. Fifty something million dollars for a Van Gogh. You know, if there is an afterlife, and if Vincent is up there watching, he's chopping off the other ear, going, "Son of a bitch! When I was alive, I couldn't sell dick!"

You know we live in such a pathetic world. It seems as if every year or so there's another new war breaking out somewhere. There was war in Sri Lanka. War in Beruit. War in Yugoslavia. In Croatia.

Sometimes I think war is God's way of teaching us geography.

Before the war in the Middle East, I didn't know what the hell a Kuwait was. I thought it was a fruit from New Zealand.

Remember when Michael Jackson wanted to buy the remains of the Elephant Man? What was he thinking?

Let me see: Michael was walking around his palace,

going, "In that corner, I just don't know. A palm tree, an end table and—naw, a dead guy. Yeah, that's it."

I believe my generation is the unluckiest ever. Anything that feels good or tastes good can kill you. Everything.

Too much salt—bad for your heart.

Too much meat—gets your heart again.

Cigarettes—lung cancer.

Everything, I'm telling you. Sex is lethal now. I don't even touch myself any more. I belong to the masturbation generation.

Hey, I'm not going to use a rubber. It's the mechanics of using a rubber that's so tiring.

First of all, you find a girl. You lie to her all night, saying, "I'll respect you." Yeah-yeah-yeah. One lie after another. Finally, you get to the special point. You know that you're going to make it. But then you have to run out of there and find that little package that you can never open at such a moment.

Your hands start to sweat. You're saying to yourself, "Holy shit," while the woman is asking, "What are you hurrying for?"

You're thinking, "Oh, baby, don't dry up on me now."

You call out, "I'll be with you in a minute."

Finally, you open it up, and you're like, Ugh, sex with a rubber isn't really sex. It's Tupperware.

And the biggest fear comes afterward, after you're finished. You ask yourself, "Oh, God, did I leave it in there?"

Because if you left it in there, you're going to have to go back in there and get it. You start apologizing. "I'm sorry. This isn't very romantic, but I believe that I left something here and I don't want you to have a kid with it in there. The kid will be born wearing a wetsuit."

You pull your hand out. You notice your watch is gone and think, Shit, now I have to go back in for that, too.

Then you pull out two watches.

And that gets you really pissed.

Anyway, safe sex confused Hispanics. To us, safe sex is locking the doors.

Frankenstein. He was a strange monster. As a kid, I never understood him. He never caught any black people. No Mexicans either. He only went after very scared white people.

Frankenstein was obviously suffering from hemorrhoids. You can tell from the way he walked, Oh, shit, let me catch somebody slow.

He never went into the ghetto. A black guy with Nikes would have run circles around his ass. "Yeah, come on, Frankie, bring your green ass over here."

If Frankenstein went into the barrio, the Mexicans would've taken those bolts right out of his head. "Well, thanks, man, we need that shit for our tires. I'm glad you showed up, man. My wheel was loose."

Paul Rodriguez

I know about crimes. My introduction to crime came when I was twelve years old. It's a true story.

My mother gave me a dollar and told me to buy a bottle of Bubble-Up at the store. Remember Bubble-Up? It was a poor man's 7-Up. Basically seltzer and sugar. We'd fake like it was the real thing. It was better than nothing.

Anyway, I went to the store and walked back to the refrigerator section where they had the bottles of soda. I got a bottle of Bubble-Up. I went back to the counter, where a dude was in the process of holding up the store. I was twelve years old. He was saying, "Shut up, old man. Give me the goddamn money."

I had this bottle of fake soda and my whole life flashed in front of me.

The robber turned to me and said, "Get the hell out of here."

So I put the bottle down.

I wonder if other people have ever had the same feelings as I did at that moment. Like your butt wants to be out of a place before the rest of you. It causes you to move funny. Parts of your body are walking at different speeds. Your butt just isn't supposed to lead. But my nervous ass was out in front.

And I was just about to hit the little electronic light that makes noise when you're shoplifting when suddenly the robber says, "Hey, where the hell are you going?"

"I'm leaving," I said.

And he said, "Well, take the bottle with you, stupid."

COMIC RELIEF

My butt swung back into place. Suddenly, I got a strut. Shit, I thought, I didn't want the Bubble-Up. I wanted the 7-Up. I took a couple of Rolo candies, too. The expensive shit. I said, "Shit, Christmas in July."

I'm sick and tired of everybody worrying about being politically correct. It's all bullshit. For instance, there are no more car thieves.

Now they're nontraditional commuters.

Homeless people are full-time outdoorsmen.

Prostitutes are sexual maintenance partners.

I'm pissed off. To this day, the only Latinos on TV consistently are the Menendez brothers. What the hell is this?

We've got to shoot our parents before we get on the television set?

I can't conceive of any reason that I would shoot my parents. Of course, they don't have fourteen million dollars.

My father heard the story of the Menendez brothers. He quit playing the lottery. He said, "Screw it, I've got twelve kids. Any one of them could snap."

For a while, everyone was talking about the Bobbits. Nice couple. She's a Latino. I know that. Latino women will sever your penis.

Paul Rodriguez

White women, they just make faces. They say, "You ain't got one."

Psychological torture, I guess.

Personally, I believe that any man who rapes a woman should have his penis severed. Now I realize that probably offends a lot of rapists out there, but fellas, you don't have anything to worry about. The ACLU will never allow it.

John Wayne Bobbit was amazing. He got his penis cut off and he was on every TV channel. If I got my penis severed, I'd be a silhouette on Geraldo. I don't want anyone to know I don't got one. It ain't going to be easy to remarry.

That story wrote itself. You didn't have to be a comic to come up with the jokes. She cut it off, threw it in an empty lot across from the 7-Eleven. They report it to the police.

"Could you describe it?" the cops ask.

"Yeah, it was white."

"Shit, it's going to be hard to find."

John Wayne Bobbit should be grateful they didn't send the canine unit out on this. My dog would've eaten as much as he could and buried the rest.

Seriously, I look at that situation like this: You get your penis severed, suddenly it is an opportunity to get something better.

I'd be on the phone to the morgue in Compton.

"Hello, yeah, anybody named Raheem fill out his donor card?"

We're all ethnically divided. Los Angeles is a city writhing in racial tension. We're a powder keg.

The whites are upset about O.J. Simpson.

The blacks are upset about Mark Fuhrman.

Mexicans?

We're not involved. We were busy cleaning the house. That's the only Hispanic there was—Rosa Lopez. And she didn't see anything. She didn't hear anything.

And she didn't make nothing.

Paul Rodriguez

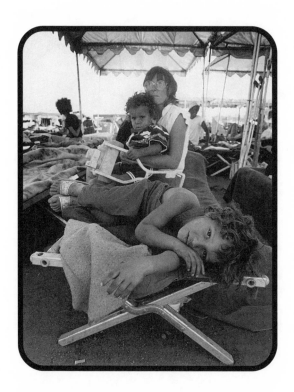

*P*eggy never thought she would be homeless. She worked hard. But after she lost her factory job, she quickly ran out of money. With no family to turn to, she also ran out of options and found herself on the street.

Peggy was among the lucky ones. She built a shelter out of plywood and plastic. It had four walls, a door and a roof. Still, she couldn't imagine herself there.

"Me, a normal person," she said. "I lived there."

Every day was a struggle for survival. Not just for food, warmth and protection. But also for her life.

"When you're out there, you just try to survive," Peggy said. "I was raped, beat up. Most of the time you just walk and walk and walk, day and night, day and night, because you're too scared to sleep because you don't know whether you're going to wake up alive."

During her third year on the street, Peggy gave up hope.

"It was really bad because I didn't know how to get out. That was the scary part. I was too scared. I didn't know where to turn or where to go.

"One night I asked God to take my life or give me a new one because I couldn't handle it anymore."

At that point, Comic Relief Health Care for the Homeless project reached out to Peggy. She was given care and respect. She got the support and love she needed to rebuild a brand-new life. And today Peggy is a mother, wife and college student.

"The help I received gave me back my self-esteem and my hope. It also gave me the sense of direction that I can do anything as long as I set my mind to it.

"Now I have my own home. I'm married. We maintain a beautiful family. We are normal people again. We have a life today.

"And it's because I was treated like I was somebody."

1-(800)-528-1000

When you walk the streets of skid row today, who do you meet? Prostitutes, drunks, drug addicts? Yes, but the shocking truth is that you also meet the new homeless, Americans forced onto the street for the first time. Single mothers, lonely teenagers, children, men who've worked all their lives but are victims of job layoffs, cutbacks and the housing crunch . . . They are the invisible poor, and they deserve our help.

—DICK VAN DYKE

I bought a new razor. The one with the sensor. I saw it on the Super Bowl, where all the major shaving breakthroughs debut.

They made it look so good in that ad. It came out of the vault in an explosion of smoke, and the guy using the razor explains how great it is. It's double bladed. The first one is psychic and the second blade is omnipotent.

They make it sound like you have to lock it in a box at night or it'll shave you while you're asleep.

I'm already one generation of razor behind.

I missed that flexo-bendy razor that you can shave a bowling ball with. In the commercial, they even say that your head is like a bowling ball. And when you're watching TV, you fall under its spell. You believe what you see. You tell yourself, "Yes, my head is like a bowling ball."

But then you get up to have a snack and come out of the fog.

You're in front of the mirror, razor in hand, going, "Hey, my head is nothing like a bowling ball. It's got a total different number of holes."

Ah, love. I thought I met this woman.

Well, I'm sure I met her, but then I fell in love with her. I thought she fell in love with me, too. Are you familiar with the situation?

I met her in another city. Everything was great. I said, "Come to California." I even bought an engagement ring.

I sat with an engagement ring, waiting for a response. I was a single guy with an engagement ring. It was like having a loaded gun laying around the house. I was frightened I'd marry somebody by accident.

But then she called and said she couldn't move to California. "I can't move away from my family," she said. "And I've been seeing another guy the whole time."

I guess everyone has had that one breakup when you just want to sit in your house for six months, smoking cigarettes and eating chicken pot pies in your underwear.

You're like, "How can people . . . fuck-fuck-fuck . . . try to work it out . . ."

Ding!

"Oh, the pie's done."

It's your one moment of pleasure. The pie loves me.

Before that I was in a relationship with a woman for five years. I hesitated to break up because I didn't think that I could meet the perfect person.

Little did I know I'd meet her and she wouldn't want to be with me.

Oh, well. I guess what goes around, comes around. I just didn't realize it would be such a short trip around.

Even though I'm single again, I'm still buying condoms.

I don't want the woman at the store to think that I've stopped having sex.

I don't really think that's any of her business. Although the condoms are piling up, so I'm going to have to have a lucky streak or think of a crafts project.

Part of the problem is that I'm not embarrassed to buy the condoms. It's not like when you first buy condoms and you mix them in with a bunch of other stuff as if you don't know that you're getting them.

I don't get that theory.

"Oh, condoms? I didn't know they were in there. But thanks guy, put them in the bag. I'll find some damn use for them."

Hopefully, I'll have the same attitude later when I have to buy really embarrassing stuff, like adult diapers.

Jake Johannsen

You kind of have to. That box is so big you can hardly mix them in with anything else, unless you're buying tractor tires.

But they hardly ever sell those two things at the same store.

I'll just throw those adult diapers in the cart without care, look the checker in the eye and say, "Those are for me, dammit.

"I've got a job to do. I'm a big boy.

"I'm peeing right now.

"Could not stop if I wanted to."

But why would you want to stop if you were protected? That's my question. It might be fun to get a box of them just for the hell of it.

What could be better?

You go into work Monday morning, talk to your boss and take a leak at the same time.

The first battle in the war on homelessness should involve educating our children and providing a stimulating environment for them to learn in.

—TIM ROBBINS

BILLY CRYSTAL
(As Lester, the owner of an L.A. chicken stand—post-riots)

This is my store. Pretty, ain't it?

I sold chicken. Barbecued chicken.

Oh, yeah, barbecued.

Not roasted. Not broasted. Whatever the hell that is anyway.

But barbecued.

The real stuff. Secret ingredients and everything.

Come on in. We're having a special on extremely well done.

It was my mother's recipe. See, nobody knows it but me and her, and she's been dead for 10 years.

I been in this spot since 1967. Before that we had a place in Watts. That one was burned down too. I remember I was so angry that my own people had burned up our store. I said, "Mom, let's not build it back up. Huh, ma? Let's not build it back up."

She said, "No son. Be cool. It's gonna get better."

Shhhittt. Yeah, gonna get better.

I knew there was gonna be trouble. As soon as I saw the videotape, you know, the first time. You think, cuz you been around, if you let them boys off, ouuu, we're gonna be in trouble. And every day for a year you see the tape. And every day they're wailing on Rodney. Two or three times a day. You'd see it even when it wasn't on. You'd keep seeing it. You'd keep thinking about it. It looked so bad for the cops who did it, you'd figure, well, that's it, this is an easy one, this is a no brainer. That's it.

But then the word got out in the neighborhood that they were moving the trial to the Simi Valley.

Ah-oh.

Then you find out ain't no black on the jury.

Big ah-oh.

Then the jury takes longer than five minutes to make a decision.

Whoa, ah-oh!

And then the news comes down. Not guilty.

Everything in me screams, "Can't be true. Can't be true. Can't be true!"

I don't know what spread faster—the word or the fires.

Blacks committin' crimes on other blacks. Burnin'. Lootin'. Families taking shit together. Saying they had a right to it. Everybody's doing it. It's free, they said.

Using Rodney King as an excuse to steal and grieve. Families stealing together. Families stealing together! All on TV for the world to see.

I cried so many tears I could've put the fires out myself.

I was looking out that front window for 30 years. Here in South Central you see nice people. That taco joint over there was once an Italian place, then it was a kosher butcher, then it was a Korean stereo joint. Now it's nothing.

And I'm watching from my window.

Nice people. "Good morning, mister. How are ya?" "Good to see ya. Hey, how you doing?"

Then I look out and see those people pulling that poor man out of the truck and beating him and I see people shooting at each other like it was the Old West. The fires started down the block, in the vegetable market that the Korean people own where I get my vegetables. Started coming fast, like a rumor about your wife. Got here real fast. Before you could say Darryl Gates, it was here and gone. Like my future. So I run out into the street for help, right, and I see all these people carrying TVs and radios and clothes and furniture and I see people throwing rocks and bottles at the firemen. The only thing I don't see is the police.

You see when people get like that you can't tell them to turn the other cheek, cuz they'd seen Rodney King. Every time he'd turn the other cheek, they'd hit it.

You can't tell people to be cool when Mike Tyson goes to jail and the Kennedy kid gets off.

Billy Crystal

You can't tell people to be cool when the Korean woman shoots a little girl and gets a talking to.

You can't tell people that.

Step on somebody's face for a while and they're going to bite your foot off.

So it's been a lot of stuff.

And then the president tells us, That's not what you're mad at. What you're really mad at is those failed liberal programs of the Sixties.

What the fuck planet do you live on?

Him and Reagan and everyone—all of them who make the space between the haves and the have-nots so damn big you can't see each other no more. And then he says, "Well, we're all in this together. We're all in it together." If that's true, get down here with a broom, George, and pick up a shovel. Pick up a broom. Pick up my life.

That's why I been cryin'.

Because the world was watchin'.

And they only see what they're told to see.

Blacks lighting fires and the world goes, "Look at them."

And I get sad. Because in my heart I know how it should go down. Maybe I'm soft. Maybe I've just been through too much. But in my heart I believe those four cops ain't all cops. The Korean woman ain't all Koreans. And the black kids who beat that man ain't all blacks.

What do we do now?

I don't know. Don't know.

What do we do now?

Insurance man was here the other day and said, "Hey Lester, you could rebuild. You could rebuild. But definitely ain't getting no fire insurance."

That's cool.

What do you do?

What do you do?

I don't know.

I know what my mother would do. She'd build. She'd build. She'd be out here with a hammer right now, if she could.

And she'd say to me now, "Son, don't forget. You've got pride. You've got soul. And . . . you've got a recipe."

RITA RUDNER

I did many other things before comedy. I was a stewardess for a while on a helicopter. For about five or six people tops. I'd ask, "Would you like something to drink?

"You would?

"Then we're going to have to land."

I had the most boring office job in the world. I used to clean the windows on the envelopes.

But now I work for myself, which is fun. Except for when I call in sick. I know I'm lying.

I have a friend who's so into recycling she'll only marry a man who's been married before.

More men are getting married nowadays. It's gotten a

little bit dangerous out there, and I guess men have to choose between marriage and death.

I guess they figure that with marriage at least they get meals.

But then they get married and find out we don't cook anymore.

I'm trying to decide whether or not to have children. My time is running out.

I know I want to have children while my parents are still young enough to take care of them.

I wonder what our children would be like. My husband is English and I'm American.

They'd probably be rude but disgusted by their own behavior.

There is truth in what they say about the sexes.
Men like cars.
Women like clothes.
I also like cars because they take me to clothes.

I suffer from peroxideaphobia. It's true.

Every time I've gotten near a blonde woman, something of mine has disappeared. Jobs, boyfriends . . . Once, an angora sweater just leapt right off my body.

Blondes have more fun, don't they?

They must.

How many brunettes do you see walking down the street with blonde roots?

I hate to generalize about things, but the police in Los Angeles. Well, it turns out Zsa Zsa was right. You have the good, the bad and the acquitted.

I think sometimes the police get carried away with those uniforms. I got a ticket for jaywalking and I was petrified. This policeman comes up to me. He has this great big helmet, big black boots, sunglasses and the belt with all the stuff hanging off of it. And he says, "Excuse me, little lady. Did you know you crossed against the light?"

I had this terrible desire to say, "No, and do you know that you look like one of the Village People?"

I hate driving. I learned how to drive when I moved to Los Angeles from New York, and I hate when people honk at me.

Unless I'm making a left turn.

Then I like it because that's how I know it's time to turn.

DENNIS MILLER

Los Angeles can be a strange place to live. Recently I got a ticket for driving in the illegal immigrant lane on the freeway. Afterward I got back in my car and continued to drive. My car was then forced off the road by aliens. I was extricated from the vehicle and led on board the mothership, where I was subjected to an extensive battery of physical testing. Many of these tests culminated in excruciatingly painful anal probes. And as I lay on the workbench and begged for my life, the lead alien tried to assuage my fears by reassuring me that most, if not all, of the tests would hopefully be covered under Clinton's comprehensive health care package.

Only man is narcissistic enough to think that a highly evolved alien life force would travel across billions and billions of light years in spacecrafts without windows.

And these extraterrestrials are so brilliant, so above it all, so insouciant, they have no need to gaze out at the celestial wonderment.

But then upon landing on our planet, we feel that their first impulse is to get into some hick's ass with a flashlight.

"All right, we touched down, Zanzar. Get the proctoscope."

What wisdom do they hope to glean from our ass?

Anyway, after the alien episode, I stopped for breakfast at the International House of Pancakes. As soon as you walk in the establishment, you catch the distinct, worldwide feel of the place. I was, I admit, completely baffled by the complex menu. So I just had the *flapjack de jour* and my syrup steward helped me select a very dry maple that was busy but never precocious.

I'm a comedian. That's my job.

Jobs are funny.

There are no hard and fast rules for making it to the top, but a pretty good rule is that if you make it to age thirty-five and your job still involves wearing a nametag you probably made a serious vocational error somewhere along the line.

The easiest job in the world has to be coroner. You perform surgery on dead people.

What's the worst thing that can happen?

If everything went wrong, maybe you'd get a pulse.

Whenever I travel I go by plane. I don't trust trains. I never have. Even as a boy, I was skeptical.

I remember those old movies where somebody would be on the train and halfway through the journey they'd reach up above the window and yank down on that brake cord. I don't want to be on any form of mass transit where the general public has access to fucking brakes. I'd hate to find out that we went off the tracks at two hundred miles per hour because Gus thought he saw a woodchuck.

Ronald Reagan was seventy-seven years old at the end of his presidency, and he had access to the button.

The button!

My grandfather's seventy-seven and we won't let him use the remote control to the TV set.

Every few years Charles Manson goes up for parole. I caught a bit of one of his hearings on the news. He showed up with a swastika gouged in the middle of his forehead. What better way to show the parole board that you've pulled your personal thing together?

The entire American system of jurisprudence is based on the premise of trial by jury. But the only way you can get on a jury is to prove beyond a shadow of a doubt that you don't know shit about the case you're about to try.

Juries don't stand a chance against these slick attorneys.

As a matter of fact, I think the reason justice is blind is because lawyers are jerking off all the time.

Is anybody else indignant that we have a legal system where you can blow your mother's head off with a shotgun, and then upon advice of your legal counsel get a neatly trimmed haircut and wear a cable-knit sweater and actually have *that* matter in a court of law?

It is an insult to the intelligence of the living and a sacrilege against the memory of the dead. We have got far too many hung juries, and not enough hung defendants.

And you know something? I know why we do this.

We do it because it allows us to fancy ourselves as more evolved, more civilized, more sensitive than the perpetrators, and I think that's a dangerous deviation from one of the core tenets of human existence—which is self-preservation.

Whether we like it or not, at some point in our personal evolution we're merely going to have to concede the fact that, pure and simple, there are some incredibly evil motherfuckers on this planet, and occasionally you have to thin the herd.

What's the Federal deficit up to now? Something like a trillion dollars. A trillion dollars and it goes up all the time.

You know what that means?

Somewhere out there, someone still insists on loaning us money.

I don't know about you, but if someone runs up a tab like that on me and I get a call from them hitting me up for more, I'm going to say, "Hey, man, what about the trillion you already owe me? That's eighteen zeros, babe. You know, I've got to see something. A deuce. The first fifty billion. Something. I'll go with you, pal, but I'm feeling a little used here."

I spent a couple of months in Paris. I lived in a really rough neighborhood, on a little street called Rue the Day.

I like Paris, but let me say something about the French people. They hate our guts. They look at us like we are one big collective Jethro bearing down on them. And you want to know something? We might be hicks, but at least we're hicks who tend to our armpits more frequently than once every time the Comet Kahotec is in the solar system. These people avoid showers like a blonde at the Bates Motel. They had to invent perfume. It was not augmentation; it was a defense mechanism.

Trust me. When Louie XVI guillotined someone, he was doing them a big favor—separating their olfactory senses from their brain stem.

I had a cab driver in Paris. The man smelled like a guy eating cheese while getting a permanent inside the septic tank of a slaughterhouse.

I said, "Hey, pal, there's an extra five in it for you if you run over a fucking skunk, okay?"

Anyone notice: Michael Jackson and George Hamilton have officially crossed lines in the pigmentation flow chart.

Oh, man, that poor bastard.

And Michael Jackson's got problems, too.

I have no doubt Michael and the little kid had jammy parties. I have no doubt they played doctor or plastic surgeon or whatever he plays. But I don't think he pulled the trigger on anything hard core. Although there seems to be a rising incidence of this in our world.

It's something I can't understand.

I know life gets tough.

I know that we all sometimes stumble down dark paths and we don't quite know what to make of life.

But if you are reading this and you ever get to the point in your life where you want to fuck or murder a kid, forget prison. You've got to kill yourself.

Just lean into the strike zone and take one for the team.

We need money because the government is a wreck. You can ask your congressman for help, but don't try to cash his check.

—BILLY CRYSTAL

RICHARD
JENI

I think it was Leo Durocher who said, "Baseball is our national pastime." And I think it was Heidi Fleiss who said, "Yeah, right."

I'm glad to be doing something positive in my work. Comedy makes people laugh and feel good, and that's important. We have a lot of problems now. Even the Catholic Church is laying people off now. They're laying off priests and going to a new voicemail confession system. 1-(800)-FESS UP.

You call in; it's all automated.

"Hello, you've reached the Catholic Church voicemail automated system. If you're a bigamist, press two now. If you're worshipping Satan, press 666 now. If you've done something you're ashamed of with a farm animal, press BAA."

"Please do not touch your private parts as this will further delay your call."

Crime is totally out of hand in this country. These days you aren't even safe in your own house with your wife. How many people remember the Bobbits? She castrated her husband—while he was sleeping! Women like that a little more than they should for my taste.

Anyway, I'm not asking why she'd cut it off. I want to know why he didn't wake up. How sound a sleeper can you be?

I've gone to bed drunk in my life, but I tell you what: if my wife is slithering under the covers at three in the morning with a miner's hat and a Ginsu, hacking away at the love gherkin, there's going to be a blip in my REM cycle.

Of course, you want to talk about crime, you have to talk about Los Angeles. It's the carjacking capital of the country.

I don't think I'm paranoid, but I'm at the point where I'm driving with the Club on.

L.A. is a sick place to live.

Earthquakes?

People aren't scared.

Riots?

Hey, that happens.

Cigarettes?

Run for your life!

Someone get a pasta salad and a motivational cassette tape.

Cigarette smoking is the most disgusting, horrible thing you can do, right? But now cigar smoking is cool.

It's to the point where women are smoking cigars.

I say, "God bless ya." Really. Whenever I'm in an intimate situation with a pretty gal, I want her to remind me as much as possible of Edward G. Robinson.

Nothing's better than a girl in a nightie, chomping on a cigar and saying, "I want you to take it off, see. Pinch my nipples. Pinch 'em hard, but not too hard. Don't hurt 'em. And I don't want to get pregnant, so pull it out, see. Okay, now scram. Scram! Ya hear what I'm tellin' ya?"

A lot of guys don't like talking about condoms, but to be honest I'm not one of those guys who whine about it.

Recently someone asked if I minded wearing a condom. "Does it bother you?" he asked.

"Mind wearing a condom!" I exclaimed. "Contraire. I prefer them."

True. Sometimes I wear six, seven, thirty-five condoms at a time. Why would I mind?

There's no difference in the sensation unless you count the total lack of any.

I wish I had one on right now. If only I had a piece of disgusting, greasy rubber, you know, just strangling the base of my dick . . .

. . with enough force to cause my eyes to fly out on springs, like someone in a Warner Brothers cartoon . . .

. . . and ripping out the pubic hair in eight different locales.

Mind?

Richard Jeni

That would be like a woman minding if someone Saran Wrapped your vagina.

Come on. Why would I mind?

I love a tight rippy feeling in the ball area. It relaxes me.

In fact, that's how I relax after a hard day. I like to get into my favorite chair, get naked, put on a fez and get out a monkey wrench. Then I start tightening that bastard right around the base of the old Johnson. Till I got a good blue bulbous thing that looks like a Farenheight thermometer going. Then I like to get out the needle-nose pliers and yank out my pubic hair in clumps.

And I'll be a monkey's uncle if I'm not sleeping like a baby in five minutes flat.

Mind?

Don't you see, it's not myself that I care about.

It's the poor little spermy men.

The one chance in their boring little lives to get out and do something incredible.

"Come on, men, we're going to make a baby! Hurry!"

"Oh, shit. Go back. It's a trap. The whole area is sealed off. There's no chance . . ."

"Will you quit pushing, asshole?"

"This sucks. I could've been somebody!"

Do you ever watch TV late at night and see those weight loss people trying to help you out? Like Richard Simmons hugging fat people.

"Hug me, fat people! I love you all. You've lost four hundred pounds. Let's show the entire nation a photo of you when you were at your fattest, lowest point! I know it's embarrassing. So what? It helps sell *Sweatin' to the Oldies*. And *Bouncin' to the Big Bands*. And *Fartin' to the Frampton Album*."

Is he helping anyone?

Is that Susan Powter woman helping anybody?

You ever see her on TV?

"Hi, I'm Susan Powter. I've lost sixteen-hundred-and-forty-three pounds. And somehow I've managed to remain totally unattractive."

Is that helping anybody?

They lie to people. They say, "It's not your fault you're overweight. You're a victim of alien obesity rays."

And I always go, "Oh, really?"

Because when I was young, I was fat. I was a fat little kid.

But after careful research and calculation, I came to the inevitable conclusion that, hey, I'm eating too much.

Somebody should be honest with the large people of America. In fact, I'll tell you who should have a late night diet infomercial. Some guy from my old neighborhood in Brooklyn. A guy who's too stupid to be diplomatic.

I can see it now:

The Joey Falco Diet Plan.

Joey, this regular guy, comes out in a T-shirt and jeans.

"Hey, folks, how ya doin'? Thanks for tunin' in.

"Listen. My name's Joey Falco.

"If you're overweight, I got a diet plan for you. It's worked for millions of people and it's called STOP EATING, YOU FAT BASTARD!

"Let me explain how it works. Food is made up of proteins and carbohydrates. Therefore, STOP EATING, YOU FAT BASTARD!

"Now some of you've been writing in and asking, 'How do I know if I'm a fat bastard?'

"Here are some ways to tell:

"'When you go to a buffet, do the waitresses put on riot hats?

"Do you find yourself winded after combin' your hair?

"When you stand up to pee, do you gotta move your chin outta the way first?

"If any of these sound like you, chances are you've become a fat bastard.

"So send only three bucks for my tape. It ain't a video-tape or nothin'. You know what it is?

"It's Scotch tape.

"Take a piece and put it over your mouth so the Twin-kies don't get in.

"Hey, try it for thirty days."

These days everyone's got something to say and they all end up on TV. There's something about giving a person a microphone. You can't shut him up. Look at the referee in football. He has his own microphone just so he can humiliate the players when they do something wrong.

The referee actually stops the whole game to point out the one guy who made a mistake and embarrass him on television in front of his mom and anybody else who might be watching. He's right out there on TV, with a little click button on his belt. He clicks it, then says, "The reason we stopped, the reason we're all hanging out on the field not doing anything, is because some people don't seem to know the rules . . . do they number 71?

"Seventy-one—I can't even look at you, you fat, waddling waste of human life. Number 71.

"What a loser!"

But you can't blame the referee. Everyone wants to be heard. He's no different. You'd do the same thing. Let's be honest. You're a referee. An ordinary guy. Not making the big money. But you have a little button on your belt. You know that for the first time in your whole stupid life the whole country will be listening to you. I'd be stopping that game every 10 minutes just to get some stuff off my chest. How often do you get the whole country to listen to you?

I'd be out there, stop the game and say, "There was no penalty. This has nothing to do with the game, the players or the National Football League. I just need to get some things off my chest. Sorry, I can't keep this up. I feel like a fraud out here. I mean, sure I'm the ref and everything, but who am I to judge these players? What if I'm wrong? Look at some of the decisions I've

Richard Jeni

made in my own life, for crying out loud. I'm 62 years old and I'm a freaking referee.

"I'll be honest with you. Lots of times when I'm out here I'm not even thinking about football. My wife's getting fat as a house. I love my kids, but if I had to do it again I'd wear a condom. It just all goes by so fast, doesn't it? One minute you're in high school, the next minute you're watching your prostate like a hawk.

"Plus the other thing that's really bothering me is that I feel like I'm a woman trapped in a man's body. I'm serious. Have you ever dressed up in your wife's underwear? Boy, you give me a pair of thong panties and some perfume and I'm one happy referee.

"Anyway, I better get back to the game . . ."

The face of homelessness is as varied as the reasons for its happening. But one thing is certain: It will never disappear unless we all get involved.

—KATHY BATES

One side of the country was torn asunder by riots, the other was ripped apart by a powerful hurricane, racial divisions made everyone uneasy, corporations started *downsizing* (translation: loyal, hardworking people were going to lose their jobs), and the government was perceived by many to be paralyzed by corruption and inertia. So when Comic Relief V aired it appeared the country needed an injection of hope and communal spirit more than ever. "Bottom line," Billy said during the opening of the televent. "It's still up to all of us."

Everyone did their part. Leona Helmsly watched from jail (maybe); Roseanne announced on stage that she had undergone an operation enabling her to have a baby (truth); Jim Carrey, then on the show *In Living Color,* explained he had survived the L.A. riots by wearing a big sign that said "Black Owned" (joke); and people around the country pledged $6.7 million (absolute fact).

There were still plenty of individuals out there who cared.

Several months later, in August, hurricanes Andrew and Iniki blasted ashore with 145 mph winds and gusts up to 168 mph. It was one of the most powerful storms ever to hit the U.S. Homes were leveled, entire neighborhoods torn apart and cities devastated. Full of faith in the public's sense of good and concern, Comic Relief quickly organized Hurricane Relief, a nine-hour concert featuring Whoopi Goldberg, Gloria Estefan, Paul Rodriguez, Julio Iglesias and many other stars. The event, held at Joe Robbie Stadium before 70,000 people, raised over two million dollars for storm victims in Florida, Louisiana and Hawaii.

Once again, Americans came to the aid of their neighbors.

"Keep it coming," Billy urged.

"Yeah," Whoopi added. "The phone lines will stay open twenty-four hours a day, seven days a week. Get one of those little yellow post-its and write our phone number down. Stick it on the refrigerator door or on your girlfriend or on your boyfriend, whatever you are. Stick it in every place you can think of. Because baby, that's what we need. We need you."

1-(800)-528-1000

When we bring a child into the world, we deliver a promise to take care of them under any and all circumstances. It's an unwritten contract. But sometimes, through circumstances or fate or choices or bad luck, we're unable to pay off the contract that binds every parent to child. That doesn't mean parents have lost sight of the dream, have discarded the contract, or stopped fighting to nurture and protect. Sometimes it just means they need a helping hand from the community.

—DIANE LADD

RICHARD BELZER & "WEIRD" AL YANKOVIC

(for best results, wear baggy pants and say the words out loud—with an urban feeling)

The Comic Relief Rap

Cut the grief
with **Comic Relief**

We put a man on the moon,
invented plastic spoons
we made a greeting card
that plays tunes

We made freeze dried food
we made Betty Boop
we made the automated, ventilated
chicken coop

163

We made a blackboard green
we made Sizzle-lean
we made a coffee bean
with no caffeine

We made Yogi Bear
we made unisex, designer label
underwear

So why can't we help the homeless?
Why can't we feed the hungry?
Help the poor people of the
country
who are homeless?

Cut the grief
with Comic Relief!
Cut the grief
with Comic Relief!

We made Velcro strips
we made microchips
we made coolwhip,
wax lips
and
no-mess drips

We made bulletproof suits
and
ladies boots

We made mutant fruit
at the institute

We made Bobby pins
we made Holiday Inns
we made My Sin perfume
and
Sugar Twin

We made Alpha Bits
We made Days of This
We made Brooks Brothers suits
for Cabbage Patch Kids

Why can't we **help** the **homeless**?
Why can't we <u>feed the hungry</u>?
Help the people who are homeless!
<u>Help the poor</u> of the country!

Cut the grief
with **Comic Relief!**
Cut the grief
with **Comic** Relief!

We made surrogate moms
we made atomic bombs
we made billions and billions of megatons

We made MTV
we made the B-1B

Richard Belzer & "Weird" Al Yankovic

We made the AC-DC
PC
and the BLT

We made a silicon tube
we made a Rubik's cube
we made a tubeless tire
and
a tireless tube

We made Crazy Glue
we made Porky's II
we spent several million dollars
making Dippity-Do

So why can't we help the homeless?
Why can't we feed the hungry?
Help the people who are
homeless!
Help the poor of the country!

Cut the grief
with Comic Relief
Cut the grief
with Comic Relief
! ! ! ! !

166

COMIC RELIEF

As a parent, the first thing you teach your child is to take care of you in old age. Next, you teach them how to tie their shoelaces, eat with a spoon, pick up after themselves, and of course you teach them their address. You tell them where they live.

But imagine how a homeless child feels when classmates ask, "Where do you live?"

And what do they say if a friend asks, "Can I come over and play?"

—MARILU HENNER

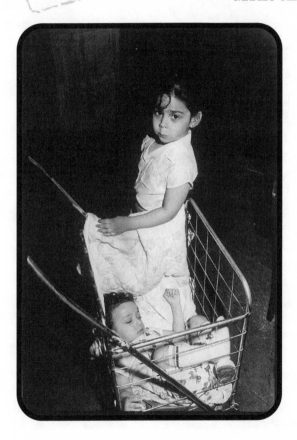

CAROLINE RHEA

I used to work in an office. They're always so mean to the new girl in the office.

"Oh, Caroline, you're new? You have lunch at nine-thirty."

I worked as a receptionist, but I couldn't get the hang of it. I kept on answering the phone by saying, "Hello, can you help me?"

It's so humiliating to go on job interviews, especially when they ask, "What was the reason you left your last job?"

"Well, I found that after I was hired there was a lot of tension in the office. You know, I found it difficult sitting on the new girl's lap."

I travel all the time in my current job as a comic, and I've found that the friendliest people are in the South.

When I'm in New York and staying at a hotel and

checking my messages, I'll call down to the front desk and say, "Hi, it's Caroline. Do I have any messages?"

They say, "Is your light on?"

"No."

But in the South when I call up and say, "Hi, it's Caroline. Do I have any messages?" the answer is different.

They say, "Yes, you do. Billy called. I think he likes you."

I just became an aunt. It's very exciting.

My sister was in labor for 36 hours. Ow. She got wheeled out of delivery, looked at me and said, "Adopt."

When my best friend had her baby she gained eighty pounds.

Oh, don't think I wasn't photographed next to her every day. I've never been thinner.

She was in total denial. Right before she had the baby, she asked, "Do you think there's any chance this baby could weigh up to eighty pounds?"

"No," I said. "I'm your best friend and I'm going to have to go with forty-five tops. And I feel that's quite a chunky baby, really."

It's embarrassing, though. Literally everyone I know is having a baby and I'm childless—except for this boy that I'm dating.

He's so young he has that new car smell.

Yummy. Fresh wax.

But they all have these incredible stories and everything I do in comparison seems inconsequential.

They say, "Well, I was in labor for eleven hundred hours. I had the baby out in the woods. And now I'm back at work full time and I'm breast feeding."

I'm like, "I bought a new skirt."

My goddaughter is so cute. She's two and a half. She saw her father in the shower and she came running out screaming, "Mommy, daddy has a tail."

Of course, I'm the evil single girl.

I had to ask, "Is it a big tail?"

Mommy's lucky.

I have a totally wonderful new boyfriend. He calls me cutie—which is short for chronic urinary tract infection.

He is so romantic.

For Valentine's Day, he gave me cranberry juice.

Dating in your twenties is totally different from dating in your thirties. In your twenties, it's fun. It's like getting a science project.

"Hey, what'd you get?"

"I got an alcoholic. I'm going to change him."

In your thirties, it's so much more to the point.

You open the door, look at the person and think, Am I attracted to you? Could I marry you?

No.

Well, it was nice opening the door.

"Next!"

I think I'm having low self-esteem about my relationship. I just failed one of those quizzes.

One of the questions was, "When is it okay to start

walking around naked in front of your new boyfriend?"

I answered, "When you want to end the relationship."

I think everyone has low self-esteem to some degree. Because no one can ever take a compliment.

If you ever give anyone a compliment, they either totally dismiss it or they confess some really horrible thing about themselves that you would never have otherwise known.

You'll tell someone, "Oh, you have a beautiful smile."

They'll say, "My back tooth is completely black."

"Oh. Well. That's a beautiful dress you're wearing."

"It was a dollar."

My mother left me a message on my answering machine. It's very sad. Neither of my parents understands how an answering machine works.

When my mother leaves me a message she's actually trapped inside the machine. It is just like a desperate cry.

"Carol? Carol? Carol? Carol? Are you there? Carol? Carol? I'm in the machine."

And my father's even worse.

He leaves me these messages: "Uh, tell her that her father called."

If asked about the possibility of losing your job, you would probably answer, "Not likely." How about your car? Your home? Your possessions? "That happens to other people," you would say. "Not me." Well, guess what? These things are happening to plenty of good people whose lives are turned upside-down by some random act of fate. In other words, sometimes the other guy turns out to be us.

—DEAN CAIN

BOB "BOBCAT" GOLDTHWAIT

Scott Baio is the Antichrist!
Scott Baio is the Antichrist!
Scott Baio is the Antichrist!
Scott Baio is the Antichrist!

I got done with my performance one night and a woman came up and said, "I really liked your act. Do you want to come to my house and do some coke?"

I said, "Yeah, yeah! I'm the guy you want wired in your apartment."

It'd be like, "What do you mean you don't have any more pretzels? Ahhhhhhh!"

I lost my job. No, not really. I know where my job is. It's just that when I go there a new guy is doing it.

I lost my girlfriend. No, not really. I know where she is. It's just that when I go to her house there's a new guy doing her.

It's been almost ten years since my wife and I pounded out our daughter. That's kind of an extremely sensitive way to say we had a child.

We pounded her out.

It was a blessed event, a wonderful, miraculous thing. But it also showed me what a self-centered dick I am. We're in the hospital and the doctor says, "Mr. Goldthwait, we're going to have to perform a C-section."

A C-section is an operation. It's a big deal. They put the woman under and then they pull the baby out through the belly.

"Mr. Goldthwait, we're going to have to perform a C-section."

Instead of going, "Oh, my God, I hope everything's okay," I went, "Oh, great, I went to Lamaze for nothing."

So I was there in the operating room when my daughter, the baby, came out of my wife's belly. Most babies are really ugly when they're born. But my baby was just beautiful. She smiled so peacefully. Most babies get their heads squeezed as they go through that Playdoh Fun Factory of life. But the doctor took my baby out of my wife's stomach. Then he turned to me and asked, "Mr. Goldthwait, would you like to cut the cord?"

And I said, "Isn't there anyone more qualified?"

I mean, come on. This doctor has good judgment? Why would they give me a sharp object around a newborn?

Scott Baio is the Antichrist.
Scott Baio is the Antichrist.
Scott Baio is the Antichrist.
Scott Baio is the Antichrist.

I watched one of my favorite TV comedies—*A Current Affair.* They showed an execution at some prison. The executioner said, "Killing a man in an electric chair is as easy for me as going to the refrigerator and getting a beer." I heard that and thought, Well, scratch that guy off my A-1 party list.

He'd be partying at my house and I'd say, "Hey, did you get my beer?" Then he'd look at me funny. "Huh? I thought you said kill your dad."

I'm a fan of the group U2. I like Bono, the group's lead singer. I once watched the group perform at a big

Bob "Bobcat" Goldthwait

stadium concert, and Bono was singing "Pride in the Name of Love," a song about Martin Luther King's assassination, and seventy thousand people were singing along. I got goosebumps. It made me wish I had that kind of relationship with an audience. I was literally crying, tears streaming down my face, and then this guy next to me says, "I'll bet you Bono gets so much pussy."

Fuck that.

"Bono doesn't get pussy," I snapped. "He's singing about peace, you bag of shit. If I see you at the Earth Day concert, I'll beat the shit out of you."

Remember the Oliver North trial? Even though years have passed, I can't figure that one out. He was dismissed from the military, right? But when he went to court he wore his uniform.

Now I've been fired from a lot of jobs, but you don't see me tooling around in my Burger King outfit.

Here's a parting thought, a kind of humanitarian thing: Please, if you ever see me getting beaten up by the police, please put your video camera down and help me.

Why does voting in a presidential election seem, at least to me, a lot like going into an adult novelty store and wondering which is going to be the least painful dildo?

Ah, well. I'm not fucking weird or nothing. And Scott Baio is not the Antichrist. And if you believe *that*, America . . .

BILLY CRYSTAL
(As Dominic Vitello)

Eddie Bruno and I went to high school together. We enlisted in 1966. We were in B Company, which was just outside Da Nang. Eddie got killed, and me, hey, I was just lucky. My name is Dominic Vitello.

I left high school for the army. Right after my SAT scores.

Come on, somebody, pay me back, all right.

Pay me back so I don't have to sleep in the train station. Pay me back so I can stop sleeping on the subway grating just because it's warm.

Pay me back.

I'm good for it.

You have my legs as collateral.

I mean, how did this happen?

This is America I'm talking about. Reagan, he walked off into the sun like a god and people forget the shit he pulled by cutting funds to the homeless. Now he can't remember either. And George, I was surprised at him. He went to combat. He got shot down. He got shot down in the ocean, right? I wonder if he remembers how he felt treading water in the ocean until he got fished out. Just bobbing there all day without knowing if an enemy ship was going to pick him up or if he was going to become a Happy Meal for some shark. I feel like that every day. And Bill, my man, he's trying. Or he would try if they let him.

This is America I'm talking about, and there's a battle out here. That's what I want to tell all of you.

The enemy is us.

The enemy ain't wearing camouflage. He don't have guns, he don't have missles and he don't have nerve gas.

He wears a suit and tie and he's got a calculator.

I'm talking straight, man. I'm not an addict. I'm not a drunk, all right?

What I am is PFC Dominic Vitello, and I'm broadcasting from my mobile home here, requesting some respect.

Slow down, people. Stop your cars. Don't walk so fast by where I've set up my makeshift camp. I ain't dug in. I'm right here on the sidewalk. Look out the window. Turn that thousand points of light into one big bright beam and you shine it on America, and you're gonna see us out there. Whole platoons of us. From Vietnam. From the Gulf. You're going to see us.

I mean, this is America I'm talking about.

COMIC RELIEF

As you sit in your home, drive home, paint your home, repair your home or just complain about your home, it's important to remember that you have such a blessing as a home. Many people don't.

To help them, you don't have to act like you care, you just have to care enough to act.

—RICHARD DREYFUSS

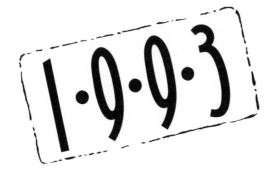

*J*eremy, *a young boy, lived in a car with his family.*

Jeremy:

"Even when the windows were closed, it was cold. We had blankets, but I had to sleep sitting up, and my back started hurting, and my neck hurt, because I had no pillow. And it was crowded, because there were six kids."

Eventually, Jeremy's family moved into a shelter.

"My friends at school say, 'Hey, where's your house? Maybe I can come over.' I say, 'I don't have a house. I live in a shelter.'

"I want to have a home to go to after school. I'd like to be able to go up to my room and do my homework.

"Sometimes the kids at school tease me about being homeless, but it isn't funny. How would they like it?

"All them kids out there are lucky. They have a home to go to. I don't."

Chris, age fourteen, never knew his father. After his mother was laid off from her job, they lost their apartment and ended up on the street.

Chris:

"It's scary, and you don't know what's going to happen. You think, Am I going to be homeless for the rest of my life? Maybe I'm not going to be able to go to school. Maybe I won't be able to make money. You want to kill yourself. That's how bad it is.

"My mom worries about me a lot. It bothers her what happens to me. She cares more about me than she cares about herself. It makes me worry about her."

Eventually, Chris and his mother were taken in by a shelter connected with Comic Relief, but that, the teenage boy knows, is only a temporary solution.

"My bed is small. There are so many people in one room. And everyone knows everyone's business.

"I don't care what people think of me, because if you care what people think you're never going to be happy. Just be yourself.

"Everyone needs to chip in and start getting involved, or [the problem] won't get any better."

1-(800)-528-1000

JUDY GOLD

I live part of the year in New York and part in Los Angeles. I have a little house in L.A. It's nice. Well, the bedroom is nice. I have french doors in the bedroom. They don't open unless I lick them.

I used to have an apartment in L.A. with roommates. That was really annoying, because my roommates had nose rings and I couldn't concentrate on a word they were saying without staring at their nostrils. They could've told me the apartment just burned down and I'd say, "Uh, did that hurt going in? Can you pick your nose?"

One of my favorite things about L.A. is this great Chinese restaurant I go to called Chin Chin. Once I went and found there had been a bomb scare earlier. Who the hell is going to phone in a bomb threat to a Chinese restaurant? Can you imagine that phone call?

"Her-ro, Chin Chin."

"Yeah, there's a bomb there. Everyone's gonna die."

"Eat here, pick up or de-riv-ery?"

"A bomb!"

"Cash or credit?"

"A b-o-m-b!"

"Steamed or flied?"

"I said, 'A bomb.' "

"Chopstix or flork?"

"BOMB!"

"Okay, thirty minutes."

You can't smoke in any of the restaurants in L.A., which pissed my friends off. I have this one friend, Patty, who has smoked like four packs of cigarettes a day for something like twenty years. Now she has that deep, gravely voice. It's so annoying and gross.

Anyway, she visited me a few weeks ago. She kept rubbing her eye.

"Judy," she finally said, "I got something in my eye. Look at it. What's in it?"

"It's a fucking tumor, Patty," I said. "Quit smoking."

Like everyone else in L.A., she is fake healthy. I was on the phone ordering from Chin Chin and she walked over to me and said, "I want steamed vegetables—-no oil."

"Did you say no oil?" I asked.

"I don't want any oil," she repeated, and then she added, "I want to also go to the gym with you. Do some cardio."

I imagined her on the stairmaster. Wheezing. And

then after lighting up a cigarette so she could feel like normal.

My mother grew up in New York, and she's one of those Jewish women who think that Jewish people are perfect. In her mind, Jews never do anything wrong. There are no Jewish criminals. It's not only unrealistic, it's pathetic.

Like when they picked up David Berkowitz, the Son of Sam, on Long Island, I thought she was going to have a heart attack.

She called me two days later and left a message.

"He was adopted. Talk to you later. So long."

She's a good mother, though, and I love to piss her off. I don't know why. It's bad. But to this day I love to get my mother mad.

If you're looking for a way to piss your mother off, here's what I suggest—and I actually did this one to my mother: Next time you're driving with your mother, stop in front of the local strip joint, put the car in park and say, "I'll be right back. I just have to run in and pick up my check."

My mother got her cataracts removed several years ago. The doctor gave her these huge sunglasses to wear. She still wears them. She thinks they are attractive. She looks like Bea Arthur as a welder.

I love her, though. I call her every day. I've actually called her from as far away as Amsterdam. Two years ago I went to Amsterdam, which is an amazing place,

Judy Gold

and visited the Anne Frank house. It was the most moving, emotional experience of my life. You walk in the house and see where the Frank family lived. It is an unimaginably small space, and the Frank family spent two and a half years there.

They couldn't make any noise all day for fear of being caught by the Nazis, which would've been the demise of my entire family. There's no way my mother could've kept her mouth shut for the entire afternoon.

"Judith, I asked you to wash that dish ten minutes ago."

Shush.

"That's right. We're gonna get caught. We're all gonna die because you couldn't wash a goddamn dish. You proud of yourself?"

My mother thinks I'm going to get killed at any moment. Anytime I walk out of my apartment in New York. But you know what? I don't think New York is that dangerous. I think people are just weird there. There are just a lot of weirdos.

Three years ago or so in the city we had this guy the newspapers dubbed the Dart Man. He was actually this mental case wacko who walked down the streets and threw darts at women's asses. So they called him the Dart Man.

My mother caught wind of this, and one day I came home to find a message from her on my machine. "Judith, wear thick clothes."

She's completely out of her mind.

And she adds, "Then the dart won't penetrate."

COMIC RELIEF

Thanks a lot, mom.

Anyway, one day I leave my apartment and go to my agent's office for a meeting. I happened to call my mother from there, because the phone call is free. We were in mid-conversation when we got disconnected. I didn't call her back right away, and I also neglected to mention that I was in my agent's office. Needless to say, she got completely paranoid. She thought we got disconnected because something happened to me in my apartment. So when I got home, I found a message from her on my answering machine:

"Judith, I didn't hear back from you. I tried to call you but you aren't answering. Where are you? I'm a wreck. I don't understand this. I'm going to call Marjorie."

Marjorie is my next-door neighbor.

"I'm going to call Marjorie and tell her to go over and find out what happened. Judith, where are you?"

And here's the clincher. Ready?

She says, "So long."

She thinks Jeffrey Dahmer has chopped my body into little pieces and she says, "So long."

Oh, well. What else is there to say?

Is there any more fun for a mother than shopping for new clothes for a newborn baby? For some parents, though—and especially single mothers who now make up a third of the homeless population—shopping for baby clothes, as well as getting food and securing shelter, are terribly frightening challenges rather than simple pleasures. But with our help, we can give them hope it won't always be that way.

—HEATHER LOCKLEAR

1·9·9·4

"I think you're going to hear so many Lorena Bobbit jokes, we're going to have a separate tote board," Billy said at the top of Comic Relief VI. "Every time you hear one, the guy who makes Ginsu knives should chip in a thousand dollars." Billy was right. There was a generous helping of Bobbit jokes. For instance: "She's having a garage sale, and all the condoms are half off." And: "After it happened, the police had an all-points bulletin that said, 'Keep your eyes out for a little dick.'" "She said he didn't satisfy her sexually before and so I want to know what she was thinking after she cut it off."

The viewing audience was equally generous with their money. By the end of the five-hour evening, the event had raised a whopping $7.8 million. In contrast to the Bobbit dilemma, it was Comic Relief's biggest night ever. In eight years, we had distributed roughly $28 mil-

lion and provided direct services to more than one million homeless individuals. But as the number of
homeless babies huddled in the backseats of cars and
families wandering city streets, hungry, ill and without
hope, continued to increase, so did our resolve to help
them out.

"The next time you see someone without a place to
sleep or without something to eat," Whoopi said, "you
just give us a call."

1-(800)-528-1000

As hospital administrators and doctors tell you, they are not equipped to deal with the medical problems of a large group of people who have no access to health services and no way to pay for the care they need. Ironically, these are the poor and the homeless, and they are the ones who need that care the most. Medical attention should be a right, not a privilege. But the need for these services far outstrips their availability. We can no longer ignore the situation. In one way or another, we're all caught up in the problem. We must all be part of the solution.

—DENZEL WASHINGTON

RICHARD LEWIS

I hope you've in love, and I hope you feel good about yourself, because I am not in love and I don't feel good about myself.

I recently broke up with this woman. Why? I felt she wasn't into me. I said, "I love you. I adore you. I worship you."

And she said, "Ain't that a kick in the head."

That wasn't enough for me.

Now she's bad-mouthing me. She's telling all our friends that she had to fake foreplay, that I gave her an anticlimax.

I'm not excited about that. Now I can't go out anymore. I have to go to a penis awareness clinic.

But you know, when it's over, it's over. And I should know.

I would get into bed and she would mentally dress me.

She got into bed at night wearing turtleneck pajamas. I wasn't thrilled about that.

She put an arm rest in the middle of the bed.

I guess I had low self-esteem. I fantasized that I was someone else, and I was happy about that.

I went out with a new woman and I said, "Look, don't take this wrong. I love you very much. Yet before we make love, can we just boil ourselves before we get into bed?"

She thought I was nuts, but I had a point.

"Look, I hate rashes. You hate rashes. Who likes rashes?"

Masturbation—right now I don't even do that anymore. Quite frankly, I'm afraid I might give myself something.

It's a sad thing. I lay in bed and say, "Richard, can't you just be friends with yourself?"

I never felt good sexually in bed. I guess it's the result of a weird upbringing. It's just hard performing in bed. When I'm making love and have an orgasm, I give away family secrets. I'm not thrilled about that. It's like at that special moment I start saying things like, "My family had a coal mine in Wyoming."

I read the *Joy of Sex,* the little instruction book. But I don't get it. You're trying position twenty-nine A. You're in bed. You're wife's holding a wok.

I can't do that.

If I ever wrote a sex manual, it would be called, *Ouch, You're on My Hair.*

Frankly, I'm two breasts away from being exactly like my mother, which is not good.

And sadly, my last shrink just retired. I'm freaked out about it. She was only twenty-four. I guess I burned her out.

The last session was unbelievable. She set herself on fire and ran out of the session going, "No *mas!* No *mas!*"

But hey, I have bad posture. I have low self-esteem. I'm unhappy.

And she said, "So?"

Well, I can blame my parents. I want to blame my parents for practically everything. After high school, I asked, "What should I do? I have no idea. Tell me what I should do?"

They said, "Run away with the circus."

That wasn't good for me.

During student government week in elementary school, I was the coroner for the day. Later, when we had freshman basketball, I was the towel boy. That was very humiliating. But just recently I was in bed with a woman, who I was really anticipating being with sexually, and, well, this will explain how screwed up I am. She said, "Don't you want to have an orgasm?"

And I said, "What's in it for me?"

Always try to find someone you love. I'm starting from ground zero. In fact, I'm reading these self-help books. Right now I'm into *Courage to Urinate.*

Richard Lewis

I should've known my last relationship was going down. I was getting cranky. I said, "Will you keep the knitting down?"

And sexually it was a nightmare. We got into bed and she said, "I'll race you to sleep."

She wanted to save her orgasm for a rainy day.

I called her breasts Mutt and Jeff.

A couple of Amish friends came over for an erection raising.

We were having problems.

Okay, so my penis has been homeless for a while now. My ex still calls every now and then. I was reminded how suddenly, for no reason, she'd talk like a pirate. She sounded like, "Aye, I don't want brunch today, matey." Of course, she was an actress and that makes a difference.

She was egotistical. We would only make love if she was on her good side.

But that whole physical thing got to me. Once when we made love I asked if she'd had an orgasm. She said, "Yeah, but I was hoping for a series."

That's sad.

This woman didn't want me, though. She didn't want me as a person and didn't want me in bed. We were once having foreplay and she asked, "What's next?"

She finally consented to having intercourse if she could combine it with learning a trade.

And when we finally were screwing, she complained I was blocking her view.

Naturally, I take some responsibility. I have a tremendous fear of intimacy. A lot of people have that. A fear of commitment. I slip in pre-nuptials on blind dates in restaurants. I'm not proud of this, but I say things like, "Oh, the shrimp's great. And by the way, everything before this I own."

I purposely studied ventriloquism so that I could throw my orgasm. I just couldn't say it.

In fact, I feel lucky just to get aroused, because my penis is usually in the shape of a question mark.

If I am lucky enough to get an erection, fortunately for me, my hard-on points to the nearest counseling center.

In all honesty, there have been times when I felt I was with the right woman. She would say, "I love you. I really love you."

I, in turn, would say, "Fine, I think we can work around it."

Ah, but you get in one of those relationships and then there's too much pressure in performing. Performance-wise, I'm sorry. Premature ejaculation—well, you know, it happens to everybody. When it happens to me, I say, "Hey, you know, it's just my way of saying that I'm happy to see you."

At my age, I'm lucky to get an erection. I'd be happy

Richard Lewis

if a flag came out with a sign that said, "Hey, thanks for the opportunity."

My problems all boil down to how I learned about sex. When I was little I asked my father the questions every boy wonders. For example, a vagina. I thought it was involved with sex, but my father couldn't even tell me. I said, "What's a vagina?"

He said, "It's an aerial view of geese."

I said, "What?"

"An aerial view of geese," he repeated.

Didn't make any sense. I wondered what that was all about.

And so I walked around, this confused virgin, muttering, "Jesus, an aerial view of geese."

But then I asked, "What's a clitoris? Everyone's talking about it."

My dad said, "It's a mouthwash."

I said, "Really? A mouthwash?"

So I've spent the rest of my life looking for three women who, by chance, happen to be walking in formation while gargling.

Which explains everything.

Everybody always asks you to give money to help this or that problem, just like homelessness. But money is only part of the solution. What really gets to the core of solving the problem is when you go out there and give people a little hope, a little understanding and a little love. As all of us know, money has never made anyone feel as good as any of that.

A little hope, a little understanding, a little love. Make that pledge today.

—LOUIE ANDERSON

SINBAD

I learned something new. Until just recently, I didn't know *they had* to take you in at the hospital emergency room.

This could change America. This could help with the high medical costs and health care problems.

You don't need a doctor.

Just go to the emergency room.

I'm not going to another doctor in my life. I'm going to show up at the emergency room.

If I want a facial or my hair done, I'm going to the emergency room.

If you're pregnant right now, forget your doctor bills. Wait till the baby's about to come and then go to the emergency room.

And go after midnight. That's when it gets real crazy.

If you've got kids, you know what I'm talking about.

Because after midnight is when the kids go into action and do their weird stuff. They put hair pins up their nose, swallow stuff and all that. But then when something happens to the kid, you don't want to take them to the emergency room.

You're too embarrassed.

You'd let your kid suffocate while you try to dislodge the toy he never should've had in the first place but inadvertantly swallowed rather than take him into the emergency room and have everybody think you're a bad parent.

I don't understand how a kid can put a toy down his throat. But it happens all the time. They get the most impossible things inside their little bodies—dump trucks, accordians and computers. You want to snatch it out of their throat so you aren't the one who looks stupid when you get into the emergency room.

Those people in the emergency room will dog you.

"What kind of parent are you?"

"It's not my fault. I ain't the one who swallowed a dump truck!"

"Yeah, but you're the parent."

They have a point, and that's why you've got to trick them.

"Look, my child's a little slow."

You know, embarrass them.

"Oh, I'm sorry," they say.

"It's okay. Just please don't make the child feel bad."

People are funny in a not-so-bright kind of way. Let me take you back to the riots we had in Los Angeles. I still think about them because of how strange the whole experience was. I'd never seen a riot like that. But that's probably because the L.A. riot was the first one ever televised like a sporting event.

We sat at home and watched TV. Like everyone else, we flipped through the channels looking for the best stuff.

"More violence on channel 9?"

"Quick, turn it! Turn it!" we yelled.

"There's fire on seven?"

"Change it to seven! Quick!"

That's how we watched.

I saw reporters drive into neighborhoods they'd never been in before in their entire life. People were looting stores. The reporters stopped them.

"Sir, why are you taking that TV?" they asked.

"I need a TV set," the people answered honestly. "My name is Bob Wynn, and I lived down the street, and I needed a TV. Hi, how you doin' America? I been looting all day. I'm kinda tired now."

That's how it was, and it was wrong.

Wrong!

If you're going to steal something, don't be seen. When the camera comes, put the TV set down. Don't give them your name and address.

But people forgot the rules.

I saw a man burn up his own store. His own security camera caught the whole thing.

This man should not go to jail, though.

If you ask me, he should go back to school. He needs an education.

The strangest thing of all was seeing National Guardsmen patrolling the streets, though it had to be even stranger for them. When you go into the Guard, you expect if war breaks out to be sent to someplace like Kuwait. But these guys were sent to Los Angeles. Can you see them talking to their kids and grandkids years from now?

"Hey, granddad, what was the war like?"

"Well, let me show you a picture. We were down there at Disneyland and it got real ugly there. Mickey almost jumped on us. We were scared."

Ah, but people keep making more people. Women keep getting pregnant, and you know what that means?

Well, I feel sorry for the husband who doesn't know what that means. Only men who've been to the emergency room with their women know.

I have. I'm a witness. And I have some advice for those men who haven't gone through the miracle of birth yet:

Do not go into the room with your wife.

If she has the baby, it's on her.

You should be there—just stand outside the door. Like in the old days.

Back then, men waited outside and they weren't considered old fashioned, insensitive or Neanderthal. There was a reason.

And the reason is you should never see your wife like that. If you do, you'll never look at her the same way again.

Not once she's had that baby and lost her mind for those few hours.

No one should see that. Only family members who grew up with her should be in that room.

Women go through different stages of pregnancy.

When they first get pregnant and nothing's showing. They've just found out, and they are all excited. "Guess what? Guess what? I'm pregnant! Yes-yes-yes!"

Then the change happens. This woman that you don't know starts to come to life. She starts putting on weight.

And yes, women, you do get big. You are big. You're having a baby! You are. Your legs swell. Your ankles swell. Your neck swells. Your whole body gets big!

So why do you make us lie?

Why do you get up real close to us, as if we'd miss something that large—you get right up in our faces—and then you ask, "Am I fat?"

"No, it's just . . . you know . . ."

"What? You can say it."

"Okay. You're pregnant."

"So I am fat."

"Well, if you know, why are you asking me? You saw yourself when you walked in here. You know you're fat."

The reason women get fat when they're pregnant has

nothing to do with the baby. It's that they keep eating stuff.

They eat all the stuff they wished they could have before getting pregnant.

"Oh, give me the ribs! And some salt. Just put some salt on the ribs. Don't worry. I'm pregnant."

Come on, ladies, don't blame that on the child. That child doesn't want ribs. No child wants a bone in its eye.

Finally you take Lamaze classes. I went. It was a total waste of time. Ain't nobody going to breathe a baby out. There's going to be a fight.

Forget Lamaze. Take a self-defense class. Take kick boxing. Learn to protect yourself in that room. Learn to cover up when your wife asks you for more ribs.

"You sure you need more, baby?"

"I want ribs. Let me have my ribs!"

I'm one to talk. Getting in shape is hard. You reach a certain age and your body doesn't react like it used to. Fat just jumps on your body.

When you're in your twenties, you can eat a whole bag of Oreo cookies. Nothing happens.

I'm now in my late thirties. I eat just one and my butt expands while I'm chewing.

I tried to lose weight with NutraSystem, and my advice is—don't. Just be fat.

When I started this woman gave me my whole week of meals. It fit in a little bag. I said, "No, this isn't going to work. I'm sorry."

So she gave me some Nutra chips and said if I got

hungry I could eat a chip. I said, "Listen, if I could eat just one chip I wouldn't be at NutraSystem.

"My problem is I like to eat!

"If you want me to eat one chip, then give me only one chip."

Then they gave me this chocolate spray. The woman said, "If you want a candy bar, just spray this chocolate in your mouth."

I had that sprayer in my mouth all the time. It was like an inhaler. Before long, people thought I had asthma.

Eventually, I made them take me to the 7-Eleven and get me a Snickers bar. Why pretend?

We're lucky. We can joke about this stuff. But then we see somebody who is homeless and we treat them as if they had a disease. As if you could catch home-lessness. People get scared of them. You don't want nothing to do with them. You're even frightened to give them a dollar. Some people actually say, "Don't give them a dollar. They'll buy something with it."

Well, so what?

It's just a dollar. So you lose a dollar. What's the worst thing that can happen to you?

I know what it's like to be broke and begging for money. I know what it's like to bury your pride, sum-mon up the courage and approach strangers for money.

"Say, man, can you give me a dollar to catch a bus back to school?"

Sinbad

After being turned down or ignored twenty times, I got crazy. I'd yell at people. I'd become confrontational.

"Hey, give me a dollar!"

That got 'em.

"JUST GIVE ME A DOLLAR!"

People react to that.

They give you a dollar as fast as they can. Not out of guilt. No, if you're crazy enough, they give it to you because it makes them feel safer.

"A lot has happened since the last time we got together," Billy said at the top of Comic Relief VII.

"Newt Gingrich proposed a law against public breast feeding. Yeah, he hates to see any kid get a free meal.

"Personal message to Pat Buchanan: Halloween's over. You can take the sheet off."

Then Whoopi chimed in: "Bill Gates declared to the world, 'I am Microsoft.' Mrs. Gates had no comment."

Robin, waiting patiently, jumped into the fray.

"Secretary of Education Jocelyn Elders resigned due to opposition to her plans to make masturbation a high school course," he said. "Damn, just when there's something I can finally teach.

"I could write the manual. It's a hands-on course, believe me.

"And it has a great final oral exam."

Funny stuff, but a lot *had* happened in the span of a year. From the Republican revolution in Congress to the Simpson trial to Michael Jackson's marriage to Elvis Presley's daughter, the country seemed in a constant state of flux. The media served up bad news daily. The spirit of optimism seemed in dreadfully short supply. But when Comic Relief VII said good night after collecting almost $5 million in pledges and revenues, it was apparent—and heartening—to realize that one thing had remained the same, unchanged despite the passing of nearly a decade since the very first Comic Relief: the willingness of Americans to help other Americans.

"I don't want a hand-out, I want a job," said Fernando, a homeless man whose family was forced onto the streets when he was laid off. "It's scary, especially when you have a family. I don't want [my kids] to have a bad deal in life. I want them to have a good education and get a good job and make a life for themselves. But when I see this happen, I'm like . . . well, sometimes people need help, they really do."

1-(800)-528-1000

ROBIN WILLIAMS

I come from San Francisco. It's nice. There are a lot of people into body piercing. They get to where they look like they've been mugged by a staple gun.

They do the whole thing: fifteen earrings here, a little towel rack there. The whole number.

Some people even have the audacity to put a little bolt through their penis. Which makes me think it must be fun at the airport metal detector.

"Will you take out your keys?

"Do you have any other metal on you? Yes? Will you take that out, too."

Just a thought: Who's going to cut the turkey this year at O.J.'s house?

My favorite character from the trial was Rosa Lopez.

"Miss Lopez, did you see him?"

"*Si*, I saw."

"What did you see?"

"Bronco."

"What was it?"

"*Blanco* Bronco."

"Who told you to say this?"

"*Señor* Johnny."

Now there's outrage in Brentwood. People are going, "No justice, no latte!"

Remember the movie *The Last Temptation of Christ?* There were people outside with signs that said, "This movie's not real."

Come here, Sparky. No movie's real.

And they had other big signs that said, "You will not get into the Kingdom of Heaven."

I looked at these people and said, "Are you going to be there? If so, then I'm not going. Don't make me be with you."

What's so offensive about a movie like *The Last Temptation of Christ?*

Nothing to me. Except that Jesus is always played by a guy who looks like Ted Nugent.

They never have a Jesus who is Jewish going, "I'm with lepers here, you bastards. I walked across the water. Give me a drink. Open the door."

And the Romans are always played by English actors.

Never real Italians. They're never real Italians going, "I'm freezing my fucking ass."

Sex is scary now.

It's like you and . . . you.

That's right. You come home and put on some music that you like, something appropriate like "I Only Have Eyes for Me."

You don't have to fake an orgasm anymore. Why? Because if it's bad, who are you going to tell? You?

You can't break up. You can't say, "All right, I'm leaving." You're attached for life. You have to stay.

In the year 2000 I think sex will be a lot different.

"Honey, I'm in the airlock now."

"Okay, Bob. Leave the sperm in the dish. I'll get it tomorrow."

We've been through some weird stuff. Like the Bobbits. A few years have gone by, but I'm still curious how you lose your dick and not notice.

Wouldn't you suddenly wake up a Ken doll?

Imagine that phone call for help and advice. "Excuse me, doctor, but I have a little blood in my urine."

Maybe he was abusive, maybe that was the problem. She called a friend and said, "He abuses me."

The friend then says, "Well, throw the prick out of the house."

Robin Williams

I know there were some women who thought she threw out the wrong prick.

They said, "She should've put the other one, the one with the head and the hands and put that in the trunk, and thrown that motherfucker out.

"Save the dick!

"That's the one you can have fun with."

Do you realize that Comic Relief has raised more than thirty-five million dollars, which is a lot of money.

But think about this: A stealth bomber costs one billion dollars.

What is a stealth bomber?

I'm glad you asked.

It's a bomber that doesn't show up on radar. You can't see it. And so because you can't see it, why, it only makes sense that you don't fucking need one.

Instead of building a stealth bomber, you just have to go out in the woods and spread some wreckage around and announce that one of them crashed. Pretty soon the Russians will go, "We'd better fucking get one, too."

Then you can build a stealth airport, a stealth army and navy and pretty soon you're not spending money anymore.

We're a trillion dollars in debt. Who do we owe this money to?

Is there someone named Vinnie calling up the President and saying, "I want my fucking money today. Put it in a bag."

Do you realize why we have arms control now?

It's because we're broke, and the Russians are broke. Before arms control, we were like two junkies arguing over a plastic spoon.

Wait a minute. Speaking of drugs. Do you realize Sigmund Freud, the father of modern psychology, used enough cocaine to kill a small horse?

He thought his mother wanted his dick.

Now people who do a lot of cocaine will read that and go, "Hey, not a bad theory." Because everyone doing cocaine thinks everyone wants their dick. The only problem is they can't find it.

I used to do cocaine. Everybody did. But now I've found something a lot scarier than cocaine.

It's called Nintendo.

That's some kiddie cocaine.

Ever seen a little kid play Nintendo? They're chanting this mantra, "Mario-Mario-Mario-Mario."

Eight hours later you ask, "How're you doing?"

They're like, "Hey, can you save some money for Pac-Man, motherfucker?"

Try this:

Put the Nintendo cartridge in backwards and then play it backwards, too. It goes, "We won the war! We won the war!"

Robin Williams

I have children, and they're wonderful. Strange and wonderful. Some parents, I know, are going "bullshit!"

I think God made babies cute so we don't eat them.

How many people do you know that you'd let shit on you, piss on you and keep you up all fucking night?

They wake up at five in the morning. I don't know what kind of drug they're on. But I'm not very good in the morning. Like when my son was little. I'd look at him smiling and all ready to go and I'd say, "Good luck."

I was out of it.

He'd smack me in the head and go, "Daddy-daddy-daddy!"

A little tiny evangelist.

"Daddy-daddy-daddy!"

I was pissing, and he was tugging at me.

"Daddy-daddy-daddy!"

So I tried to be a good parent.

Which is to go downstairs and put on a videotape.

"Let's go downstairs," I said. "Daddy loves you. Okay, let's put on *Aladdin*. What a nice thing to put on.

"And now Daddy's going to go over here and pass out on the couch.

"Oh, God, you want some waffles?

"Oh, my God, daddy put on *Debbie Does Dallas*. Oh, bad tape. Oh, honey, are you? Sweetheart? Oh, you're in the microwave! Bad place.

"Okay, give daddy a fucking break.

"Here's the secret word for today—mommy."

Why Comic Relief?

Because ten years after the first Comic Relief:

- Between five and almost ten million people, including children, can say they have experienced homelessness.

- More than 500,000 people in this country are without a home on any given day.

- Requests for emergency food, health care and shelter are still on the rise, particularly among homeless families.

- Almost forty percent of the homeless are families with children.

- Homelessness can happen to anyone, and it

does, with unemployment or job-related problems singled out as the leading cause.

- Other reasons for homelessness include domes-
tic violence, drug addiction and family crises.

Why Comic Relief?

Because in ten years we have distributed more than
$35 million and aided more than one million homeless
individuals.

Why Comic Relief?

Because where there's laughter, there's hope.

1-(800)-528-1000

CREDITS

Comic Relief I-VII:

Kareem Abdul-Jabbar, Andre Agassi, Danny Aiello, Kimberly (Miss America) Aiken, Jason Alexander, Steve Allen, Kirstie Alley, Morey Amsterdam, Harry Anderson, Louie Anderson, Another Bad Creation, Christina Applegate, Tom Arnold, Bea Arthur, Angela Bassett, Justine Bateman, Kathy Bates, Amanda Bearse, Richard Belzer, Daniel Benzali, Candice Bergen, Larry Bird, Anne Bloom, Elayne Boosler, Mayor Tom Bradley, Danny Breen, Larry Brown, LeVar Burton, Brett Butler, Sid Caesar, Dean Cain, Kirk Cameron, Tisha Campbell, John Candy, Drew Carey, George Carlin, Art Carney, Jim Carrey, Dana Carvey, Cher, Margret Cho, Henry Cisneros, Imogene Coca, Natalie Cole, Dabney Coleman, Michael Colyar, Peter Cook, Bill Cosby, Dave Coulier,

Crenshaw High School Elite Choir (Sister Act), Billy Crystal, Mark Curry, Jane Curtin, Bill Dana, Tony Danza, Michael Davis, Danny DeVito, Mayor David Dinkins, Michael Dorn, Fran Drescher, Richard Dreyfuss, Rick Ducommon, George Duke, Robin Duke, Faye Dunaway, Dick Van Dyke, Anthony Edwards, Hector Elizondo, Chris Elliot, David Faustino, Firesign Theater, Joe Flaherty, George Foreman, Michael J. Fox, Johnathan Frakes, Dennis Franz, Cast of *Friends*, Estelle Getty, Judy Gold, Whoopi Goldberg, "Bobcat" Goldthwait, Marga Gomez, A.C. Green, Ellen Greene, Dick Gregory, Mary Gross, Robert Guillaume, Arsenio Hall, Kadeem Hardison, Ron Harper, Woody Harrelson, Allen Havey, Goldie Hawn, Heavy D & the Boyz, Marilu Henner, Pee-wee Herman, Howard Hesseman, Charlton Heston, Dustin Hoffman, Bob Hope, David Hyde Pierce, Bo Jackson, Victoria Jackson, Al Jarreau, Richard Jeni, Jake Johannsen, Davey Johnson, Madeline Kahn, Dr. Katz, Michael Keaton, Ted Kennedy, Kid 'N Play, Kids in the Hall, Alan King, Robert Klein, Don Knotts, Diane Ladd, John Larroquette, Tommy Lasorda, Queen Latifa, Norman Lear, David Leisure, Jay Leno, Sugar Ray Leonard, David Letterman, Eugene Levy, Jerry Lewis, Richard Lewis, Wendy Liebman, Heather Locklear, Shelly Long, Jon Lovitz, Bill Maher, Howie Mandel, Rose Marie, Cast of *Married with Children*, Penny Marshall, Andrea Martin, Walter Matthau, Rue McClanahan, James McDaniel, Gates McFadden, Audrey Meadows, Kevin Meaney, Larry "Bud" Melman, Carlos Mencia, Dennis Miller, Paul Mooney, Demi Moore, Dudley Moore, Mary

Tyler Moore, Howard Morris, Jim Morris, Kathy Najimi, Kevin Nealon, Bob Newhart, Laraine Newman, Catherine O'Hara, Ed O'Neill, "Super Dave" Osborne, Rick Overton, Gary Owens, Stuart Pankin, Tom Parks, Jane Pauley, Minnie Pearl, Penn & Teller, Rosie Perez, Joe Pesci, Michael Peters, Joe Piscopo, Kevin Pollak, Tom Poston, Paula Poundstone, Gilda Radner, Harold Ramis, Joyce Randolph, Carl Reiner, Rob Reiner, Paul Reiser, Caroline Rhea, Don Rickles, Pat Riley, Mayor Richard Riordan, Joan Rivers, Tim Robbins, Chris Rock, Rockettes, Paul Rodriguez, Roseanne, Rita Rudner, Bob Saget, Susan Sarandon, Fred Savage, Tom Scott, Katey Segal, Doc Severinsen, Paul Shaffer, Gary Shandling, Craig Shoemaker, Pauley Shore, Martin Short, The Simpsons, Sinbad, Marina Sirtis, Bobby Slayton, Sounds of Blackness, Brent Spiner, Cast of *Star Trek*, Shadoe Stevens, Jon Stewart, Sharon Stone, Raven Symone, Jeffrey Tambor, Judy Tenuta, Alan Thicke, Marisa Tomei, Dick Van Dyke, Jim Varney, Marsha Warfield, Denzel Washington, Jeff Wayne, Lucy Webb, George Wendt, Suzanne Westenhoefer, Slappy White, Robert Whul, Lee Wilkof, Robin Williams, Lester Wilson, Steven Wright, "Weird" Al Yankovic, Henny Youngman, Bob Zmuda.

PHOTO CREDITS

Title Page, Billy Crystal, Whoopi Goldberg, and Robin Williams: Andy Hayt/HBO

Page xvi, Bob Zmuda with Billy, Whoopi, and Robin: Bonnie Schiffman/HBO

Page 7, Billy, Whoopi, and Robin at the House of Ruth: Terry Ashe/HBO

Page 13, Comic Relief I: Robert Landau

Page 18, Gary Shandling: Graig Blankenhorn/HBO

Page 24, Elayne Boosler: Ken Sax/HBO

Page 34, Woman with children on cot: Jay Kaufman

Page 39, Comic Relief II: Robert Landau

Page 44, Louie Anderson: Randee St. Nicholas/HBO

Page 52, Paula Poundstone: Randee St. Nicholas/HBO

Page 63, Family in van: Jay Kaufman

Page 68, Bill Maher: Andy Hayt/HBO

Page 74, Bob Saget: Janet Vanham/HBO

Page 83, Comic Relief III: Mark Sennet

Page 88, Steven Wright: Tony Costa/HBO

Page 94, Whoopi Goldberg: Anthony Neste/HBO

Page 100, Whoopi Goldberg: Andy Hayt/HBO

Page 101, Comic Relief IV: Ken Sax/HBO

Page 106, Paul Rodriguez: Janet Vanham/HBO

Page 117, Child lying on cot: Jay Kaufman

Page 122, Jake Johannsen: Patrick Harbron/HBO

Page 128, Billy Crystal as Lester: Andy Hayt/HBO

Page 134, Rita Rudner: Patrick Harbron/HBO

Page 138, Dennis Miller: Anthony Neste/HBO

Page 145, Bob Zmuda with President Bill Clinton, Vice President Al Gore, Willie Nelson, and friends: The White House

Page 146, Richard Jeni: Janet Vanham/HBO

Page 157, Comic Relief V: Ken Sax/HBO

Page 162, Richard Belzer and "Weird" Al Yankovic: Robert Landau

Page 167, Children in shopping cart: Mary Bloom

Page 168, Caroline Rhea: Brian Fitzgerald/ABC

Page 174, Bob "Bobcat" Goldthwait: Ira Margolin/HBO

Page 180, Billy Crystal as Dominic Vitello: Robert Landau

Page 185, Robin Williams signing autographs for family: Maryanne Russell/HBO

Page 190, Judy Gold: Janet Vanham/HBO

Page 197, Comic Relief VI: Ken Sax/HBO

Page 202, Richard Lewis: Janet Vanham/HBO

Page 209, Bob Zmuda and Shelley Long presenting a check to Chicago Health Care for the Homeless project: Waldemar Reichert/Imagine Inc.

Page 210, Sinbad: Janet Vanham/HBO

Page 219, Comic Relief VII: Jim Hagopian

Page 223, Marian Wright Edelman, Senator Edward Kennedy, and Whoopi Goldberg: The White House

Page 224, Robin Williams: Andy Hayt/HBO

Page 231, Young girl: Jim Kaufman

Page 240, Billy, Whoopi, and Robin: Andy Hayt/HBO

Comic Relief would also like to thank Bob Green/HBO, Jeff Kravitz, Michelle Laureta, and Bob Ware.

Photo **Credits**

Photo Credits